SCOTLAND

THE NATIONAL CYCLE NETWORK

SCOTLAND
THE NATIONAL CYCLE NETWORK

HARRY HENNIKER

MAINSTREAM
PUBLISHING

EDINBURGH AND LONDON

Reprinted, 2007

First published in Great Britain in 2000 by
MAINSTREAM PUBLISHING COMPANY (EDINBURGH) LTD
7 Albany Street
Edinburgh EH1 3UG

ISBN 9781840188554

Revised and updated 2004

A catalogue record for this book is available from the British Library.

Maps drawn by the author using a vector graphics drawing package. Maps manually re-drawn from
out of copyright editions of the Ordnance Survey One Inch Map supplied in photocopied form by
the National Library of Scotland and updated by direct observation and with Garmin GPS software.
Heights on maps taken with a Thommen Altimeter.

Typeset in Janson Text and Gill Sans
Printed and bound in Great Britain by
William Clowes Ltd, Beccles, Suffolk

CONTENTS

FOREWORD

When Sustrans set out to create the National Cycle Network, we had one objective in mind – to popularise cycling as we travel into the twenty-first century.

For all its convenience and style, the motor car has defects which we cannot forever ignore – its sheer consumption of resources, its dead weight on our towns and countryside, and its diminution of our independence, health and fitness.

For devotees of the bicycle, this is all very frustrating, for nothing matches the efficiency and the freedom of the cycle. Harry Henniker's book shows just how, even if you haven't cycled for many years, you can now get out into the wonderful Scottish countryside by using the National Cycle Network. The Network will lead you out through the towns and give you fresh confidence to start off. Now over 1,600 miles long in Scotland, the project keeps going as fresh routes are developed, and we hope that it will become a powerful catalyst for change towards a more sustainable form of transport.

As well as writing this definitive guide, it should not be forgotten that it was Harry and his colleagues in Spokes, the Edinburgh-based cycling group, who persuaded the Scottish Office to commission studies to start work on the routes in 1984 and also convinced Edinburgh to back the historic voluntary task of building the Pilton path in June '86. Without that initiative there would be no National Routes in Scotland for us to enjoy today.

Of course, we will not be satisfied until cycling doubles and doubles again to reach the 10 per cent of all journeys enjoyed in Sweden, which surely has colder winters, and the 16 per cent proportion in Switzerland, which must be more mountainous. For sheer variety, for great towns and wonderful scenery, Scotland is a cyclists' paradise, which is now all the more accessible on the National Cycle Routes.

John Grimshaw,
Chief Engineer and Director of Sustrans

ACKNOWLEDGEMENTS

I'd like to thank everyone at Sustrans for all the help they have given me in compiling this book. In particular I'd like to thank John Grimshaw for his encouragement when I first suggested doing the book and for writing the foreword. I should also thank Tony Grant and everyone at the Edinburgh office of Sustrans for reading over the manuscript and looking at the maps. This has been a big help, but I should say that if there are any errors these are my responsibility.

Thanks also Sustrans North of England for help with the route near Carlisle.

Thanks to Sally Harrower for her drawings, which never fail to raise a smile; Dave McArthur for riding with me during some of the initial research and Alan Beal for his piece on Dundee. Also to Bill Campbell and everyone at Mainstream.

THE AUTHOR WITH A GROUP OF CYCLISTS DURING A SPOKES CYCLING WEEKEND. FOR MORE INFORMATION ABOUT SPOKES, AND THE BIKEBUS TRANSPORT SERVICE, SEE THE APPENDIX.

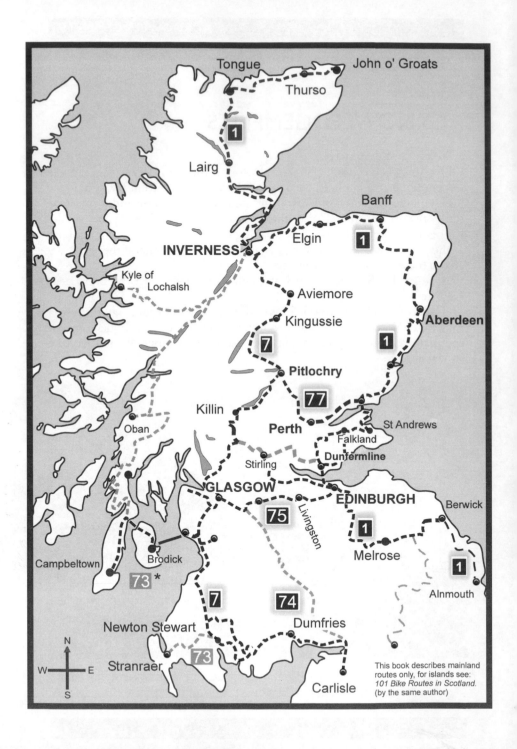

This book describes mainland
routes only, for islands see:
101 Bike Routes in Scotland.
(by the same author)

USING THE CYCLE NETWORK

The map opposite shows the Sustrans numbering scheme for the Cycle Network in mainland Scotland. The Millenium Routes, shown in red, are the ones that will be up and running in 2004 and are included in this book. The other routes, shown in grey, will be completed later.

You can expect the Millennium Routes to be fully signposted, but you shouldn't rely on the signs entirely. After all, between Glasgow and Carlisle alone there are hundreds and hundreds of signs; it only needs one to be missing and you might go sailing off in the wrong direction without realising you have a problem. Keep the book (or map) handy and check where you are as you go along.

Sustrans, local authorities, groups of volunteers, cyclepath rangers and various other groups will be working to improve the Network over the next few years so you can expect to see some changes.

If there are route alterations these will be signposted, and perhaps will already be on the maps, with a note: 'Due to open later'. If an improvement is not signposted, Sustrans hasn't negotiated access yet, so don't cause problems by trespassing.

Some of the routes shown in grey that are due to open later are being worked on at the moment, so they may be partially signposted. There is of

ON MAP OPPOSITE

NCN Route Number **75**

Selected Railway Stations ●   Place without railway station ●

Route open from 2003   Forecast route (not fully open)
▬▬▬▬▬▬▬   ▬ ▬ ▬ ▬ ▬ ▬ ▬ ▬ ▬ ▬

ON DETAILED MAPs

Route mostly on public road   Route mostly away from motor traffic
▬▬▬▬▬▬   ▬ ▬ ▬ ▬ ▬ ▬ ▬ ▬ ▬ ▬ ▪

course no reason why you shouldn't explore these routes where they run along back roads etc. – apart from the fact that the maps haven't been produced yet.

ABOUT THE CYCLE NETWORK

Besides writing books like this I run a business taking people on cycling trips in Scotland. Occasionally I get groups from North America. Of course I take them to the prettier parts of Scotland; the Scotland they wish to see is mountains, tartan, clans, heather and the romantic, failed '45 Rebellion.

The Cycle Network does go through beautiful scenery with associations of that sort, but the Scotland you will see is much more than that: ships built on the Clyde; new transport links by canal and rail; the story of a people hammered on the anvil of the original Industrial Revolution. The Cycle Network is in some ways a link between Scotland's past and future. It finds a new use for disused railway lines and in doing so you get a unique view of the past and perhaps a glimpse of the future.

The routes are very varied – on one section you might see a pine marten and red deer, on another a shipyard by the Clyde. What you won't see is motorway service stations with hordes of people.

The Network provides quiet routes for cyclists using three different methods: traffic-free paths, protected sections on roads and suitable back roads. By far the greater part of the Edinburgh to Glasgow route, for example, is on traffic-free paths. In quiet rural areas like Dumfries and Galloway, a higher proportion is on back roads. You can expect more and more of the Network to be completely traffic-free as time goes on.

WHAT TO TAKE WITH YOU

Obviously you'll need a bike, any kind of bike will do, the only thing that's really important is that it's reasonably reliable and the right size. If you're only out for an hour or two perhaps it matters less, but some way of carrying small amounts of luggage is necessary. At a minimum you'll need a waterproof jacket, a bicycle pump and a puncture repair kit, plus the means to remove a wheel.

Some food and a drink is a good idea as cycling makes you hungry. Occasionally people say 'There's no point in me taking a puncture repair kit, I don't know how to use it anyway'. The answer to that is without a puncture repair kit you've no chance at all and it's a long walk back!

Obviously for longer trips you need to go into things a bit more carefully, otherwise you could be hauling lots of useless stuff up the hill and lacking vital equipment if something goes wrong.

TOOLS

Many people carry multi-tools, a sort of cyclist's Swiss Army knife, instead of carrying spanners and all the rest separately. Whatever tools you have, they need to be appropriate to the bike you're riding. For example, if your bike has quick release wheels you won't need to carry a spanner to undo the wheel nuts as there won't be any.

The basics for a day trip or longer are: allen keys to fit allen bolts, a chain tool, puncture repair kit, spare inner tube, slot and crosshead screwdriver, small adjustable spanner, tyre levers and bicycle pump.

For a longer tour of a week or so you might also like to take: a bottom bracket tool, freewheel extractor, some oil or lubricant, spare cable inner wires and a cone spanner. If you don't know what most of these are don't worry about it – there are bike shops near the routes and if your bike is reasonably new you are unlikely to need them.

WATERPROOFS

A waterproof jacket is essential as the main characteristic of Scotland's weather is its changeability. You don't need anything fancy in summer but it should be waterproof. You also need something more than just a T-shirt to put under it. From October to April, or on longer trips, you should probably be thinking about waterproof overtrousers and warm cycling tights, which brings me on to:

CYCLING CLOTHING

Not that long ago most people used to cycle in their ordinary clothes. You don't have to buy specialist clothing but jeans are a bad idea – they are horrible when wet and the seam under the bum becomes uncomfortable after a time. Tracksuit bottoms are OK, though they may get dirty from the chain. Something tapered at the ankle is ideal.

Padded cycling shorts or cycling underwear make long rides more comfortable. Above the waist several thin layers enable you to regulate your temperature easily and something windproof is useful.

Shoes need to have soles you don't feel the pedals through. If buying cycling shoes you need to consider them in conjunction with the type of pedals you'll be using. Trainers are usually fine.

I'd be sorry if cycling helmets ever became compulsory, but I recommend you use one all the same. Get one that's the right size and is comfortable or you'll tend not to wear it. It's important that you don't get too hot with it on, so choose a design with lots of ventilation.

The strap should be snug under your chin. If you can take a big bite out of a Mars bar with your helmet on it's too loose. The price of helmets has come down recently so that's no excuse. If you damage your helmet replace it – you can't replace your head.

CARRYING LUGGAGE

The best way is in panniers attached to a pannier frame on your bike. Rucksacks are a bad idea, though bum bags / pouches around your waist are useful for carrying money, keys etc. The way to carry a map is in the transparent pocket of a handlebar bag, or in a waterproof map-case attached to the handlebars. This book is designed for this. Handlebar bags are only suitable for lightweight items.

PREPARING YOUR BIKE

You might not be a bike mechanic but there are a few obvious checks you can do before setting out – get into the habit of doing these. They only take a few moments.

TYRES Make sure the tyres are pumped up. They should feel nearly brick-hard. If you can make an indentation in them with your thumb nail they are too soft and you are more likely to get a puncture. You can get tyres with a kevlar puncture-resistant lining nowadays and these are excellent for cycling in urban areas where you might encounter broken glass.

CHAIN It should be oily; special chain lube is ideal but any old oil will do.

BRAKES Check these by trying to push the bike while pulling the brake hard – you shouldn't be able to. If they don't work it could be because of dirt or oil on the wheel rim, or you might need new pads or a new cable.

CABLES Look for any broken strands of wire – even one broken strand means the cable will break very soon. Cables should move freely. Modern bikes have cable stops that enable you to unhitch the cable outer and slide it along to lubricate the whole cable.

NOISE If there is anything loose, or if you hear an unusual noise, check it out – you might save yourself a long walk. One noise you do need is the ting from a bell to warn pedestrians.

SADDLE This should be at the right height – your leg should be nearly straight at the bottom of the pedal stroke or you'll find climbing hills difficult. Different saddles are available for men and women.

GETTING TO THE START (AND GETTING HOME)

Probably there is part of the National Cycle Network quite near you, for 90 per cent of the population of Scotland live within cycling distance of part of the Network and very many people live just a couple of miles away. Of course, eventually you might get bored with just your own local bit, or you might decide to have a cycling holiday. If so you'll need some form of powered transport to take you where you need to be.

TRAINS National Cycle Network routes are great from the point of view that many start and finish at railway stations. Don't automatically assume there will be space for your bike on the train, as some can only take a few bikes. Phone to check and if necessary reserve a space in advance. (See Appendix for numbers.)

The situation is easier in the west of Scotland in the area covered by Strathclyde Passenger Transport. I've usually found that you can hop on and off trains with a bike there no problem. Of course where there are frequent local services not getting on the first train that comes along isn't a big disaster, there will usually be another one along shortly. This situation doesn't apply on trains serving such places as Fort William and Thurso – services are usually infrequent in the Highlands. Train stations are indicated on the maps with a red dot.

BUSES Buses in Scotland don't usually carry bikes. This isn't invariably the case, sometimes you'll meet the odd driver who will oblige, particularly in the remoter parts, but this isn't any help when planning a trip.

If you live in Edinburgh and want to get around Scotland with your bike you might be interested to know about the *Spokes BikeBus*. This is a voluntary transport service for cyclists operated by Spokes, The Lothian Cycle Campaign. They run cycling weekends and the occasional longer trip. (See: www.bikebus.co.uk)

CARS Sustrans is not very enthusiastic about cars. Sustrans is short for sustainable transport and they say they are pro-bike rather than being actually anti-car. If you do have a car you might want to use it to get to the start of your bike ride. The main problem with this comes at the end, when you find that your car is in the wrong place. Solutions might be: getting someone to drive you, doing a circular route, returning to your car by public transport. None of these is ideal – it's better to get the train.

TAKING CARE (POSSIBLE HAZARDS)

What? Hazards on National Cycle Routes? I thought there weren't a lot of cars! Well, on minor road sections you will meet a few cars, but they are not the main source of danger.

PEDESTRIANS Even the dedicated cyclepaths are shared with pedestrians and in fact Sustrans advertise them as being suitable for people in wheelchairs. Having a bell is superior to merely shouting, but once you've used it to warn people don't forget to use your voice to thank them if they give way.

Urban sections often have people walking dogs on them. Dogs can be unpredictable and sometimes when you get close you realise that the dog is attached to the person by an extending lead, so slow down.

Toddlers can be unpredictable too, and parents tend to be even more protective of their toddler than a dog. The key to successful mixing with pedestrians is to be considerate, don't come up silently behind people, thank them if they stand aside, and remember this busy bit of the route will enable you to get to the quieter rural section. It isn't a big disaster if you can't race along at 15mph.

PUNCTURES These have a variety of causes and often you can take preventative action, saving yourself a lot of trouble. In rural areas the major cause of punctures is thorns. Many quiet rural roads have thorn hedges. This is not usually a problem as the thorns are firmly attached to the hedge. The problem arises when the hedge is cut and the road is covered with trimmings. The thorns can instantly penetrate a normal cycle tyre – I've seen inner tubes with 12 punctures in them, completely immobilising experienced cyclists with all the correct repair kit. Moral: if you see hedges being trimmed by a tractor with a big hedge clipper, stop. Wheel your bike carefully past and remove any thorns by hand before cycling on.

The other major cause of punctures is broken glass. This is mainly a problem in urban areas, especially where cycle routes pass under bridges. Councils, Sustrans rangers etc. do take action to sweep this up but they can't be everywhere at once. Worn tyres are much more likely to get punctures from glass. Tyres with a Kevlar anti-puncture bead are fairly immune to punctures from glass and even resist thorns to some extent.

Of course not all punctures have external causes – badly fitting spokes, poor rim tape and badly fitted tyres can cause punctures too.

SECURITY PROBLEMS Be aware that you are more likely to have problems protecting your bike, luggage etc. in certain areas. You should always have a bike lock and secure your bike wherever you are, but in urban areas you may need a big heavy bike lock, while in most rural areas almost any lock will do.

Just locking your bike to a solid piece of street hardware and piling in to the café is fine, but what about your luggage? I wouldn't dream of leaving it on my bike if I was in an urban area that I was unfamiliar with. Sometimes you can lock your bike up so it is visible from where you're sitting in the tea room, but of course you have to remember to look at it occasionally. Mostly this sort of stuff isn't a big problem, but what I'm saying is that Sustrans cycle routes go everywhere, so look at where you are and act appropriately.

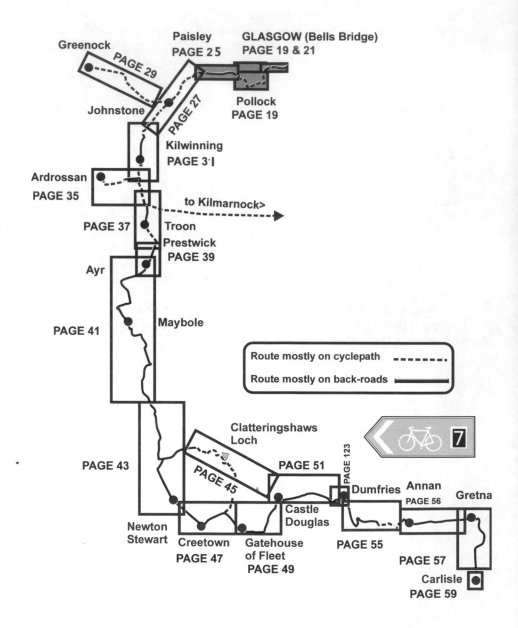

Greenock

PAGE 29

Paisley
PAGE 25

GLASGOW (Bells Bridge)
PAGE 19 & 21

Johnstone

PAGE 27

Pollock
PAGE 19

Kilwinning
PAGE 3·1

Ardrossan
PAGE 35

to Kilmarnock>

PAGE 37

Troon
Prestwick
PAGE 39

Ayr

PAGE 41

Maybole

Route mostly on cyclepath - - - - - - - -

Route mostly on back-roads ▬▬▬▬▬▬

Clatteringshaws
Loch

PAGE 45

PAGE 51

PAGE 123

Dumfries

Annan
PAGE 56

Gretna

PAGE 43

Castle
Douglas

PAGE 55

Newton
Stewart

Creetown
PAGE 47

Gatehouse
of Fleet
PAGE 49

PAGE 57

Carlisle
PAGE 59

7

2

GLASGOW–CARLISLE
(LOCHS AND GLENS SOUTH)

TOTAL DISTANCE – 193 MILES (PLUS 19 MILES JOHNSTONE TO
GOUROCK AND 7 MILES KILWINNING TO ARDROSSAN).
FOR GLASGOW TO CARLISLE START AT PAGE 18
FOR CARLISLE TO GLASGOW START AT PAGE 61 AND WORK BACKWARDS

INTRODUCTION

This route divides into two parts, a relatively populated section between Glasgow and Ayr, and a quiet rural section between Ayr and Carlisle.

The Glasgow to Ayr section is less hilly and much of it is on dedicated cyclepaths, mostly on disused railway lines. Some parts are on quiet back streets. Where you have to cross a busy road there is usually a light-controlled crossing. Even though much of the northern part of the route is in urban areas, a lot of it still passes through parks and farmland. The route around Pollok Park is quiet for example, and the railway path section between Johnstone and Kilbirnie is quite pretty and great for children.

Between Ayr and Carlisle the route passes through South Ayrshire and Dumfries and Galloway. 'Scotland's surprising south-west' is what the local tourist board used to call it and this slogan is surprisingly apt. It certainly surprised me when I first started cycling there – the hills might not be quite as big as in the Highlands but it isn't obvious looking at them. What this area does have is a great network of quiet rural roads and Sustrans has chosen some of the best.

Much of the route is in Galloway Forest Park, a huge area with some big hills, over 150 lochs and 300 miles of rivers. The Solway coast is quite lovely too, a haven for birdlife and plenty of historic buildings and castles to look at. The small towns all have their own character and there are plenty of cozy pubs and tea rooms. At the time of writing the route included a half-mile section on the busy A75 just south of Newton Stewart; this is to be improved but it may be a year or so before this happens. Bear in mind that parts of the route are very hilly – so don't take too much luggage. Be sure to take your waterproofs!

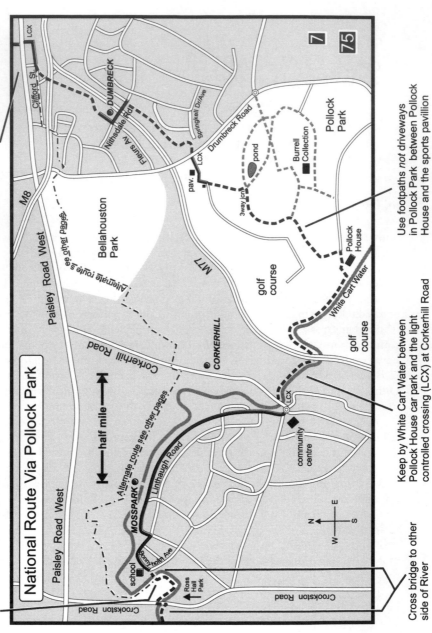

National Route Via Pollock Park

Pollock and Bellahouston routes diverge at a footbridge over White Cart Water near a nursery school

Pollock and Bellahouston routes diverge at the junction of Clifford Street and Gower Street (both routes cross M8 on footbridges)

Use footpaths *not* driveways in Pollock Park between Pollock House and the sports pavillion

Keep by White Cart Water between Pollock House car park and the light controlled crossing (LCX) at Corkerhill Road

Cross bridge to other side of River

7

75

LCX

LCX

DUMBRECK

Nithsdale Rd

Fleurs Av

Springkell Dr/Ave

Drumbreck Road

pav.

LCX

3way jct

pond

Burrell Collection

Pollock Park

Pollock House

White Cart Water

golf course

golf course

M8

Paisley Road West

Bellahouston Park

Alternate route see other pages

M77

Corkerhill Road

CORKERHILL

half mile

Alternate route see other pages

Linthaugh Road

LCX

community centre

MOSSPARK

Sunnyholm Ave

school

Ross Hall Park

Paisley Road West

Crookston Road

Crookston Road

Crookston Road

N E W S

BELL'S BRIDGE – POLLOK PARK – ROSS HALL PARK

This is the usual mixture of quiet back streets, paths in parks, and specially-built sections to avoid busy roads. The route starts at Bell's Bridge near the SECC in central Glasgow (map next page). Until the 1960s this area would have been crowded with ships – the SECC is in fact built on what was once the Queen's Dock. The Finnieston Crane, which used to load steam locomotives on to ships for India, China and the USA, is a reminder of that time. It makes Bell's Bridge quite easy to find.

A major feature of Pollok Park is The Burrell Collection; this is housed in a new building opened in 1983. It consists of a world-famous collection of textiles, stained glass, furniture, ceramics, art objects and pictures. It was gifted to Glasgow by Sir William and Lady Burrell when Sir William died at the age of 97. It was nearly 40 years after his death before Glasgow managed to find a site that met the terms of the bequest but the building is remarkable. There is a temporary exhibition gallery, a nice restaurant and a shop. It's open all year and admission is free (0141 287 2550).

The park itself was donated to Glasgow by the Maxwell family, who owned it from 1269 to 1966 and it's quite a peaceful place in the middle of the city now. Pollok House is also open to visitors. The homely interior is a good setting for a fine collection of Spanish, Dutch and British paintings (Blake, Hogarth, Goya, El Greco and Murillo). The formal gardens around the house are beautiful.

The route north-east of the park is mostly specially built cyclepath; the only points where you need to take some care are at the park exit where there is a pelican crossing to the cyclepath and at Drumbreck where the route crosses over the M77 on Nithsdale Road.

West of the park the route is on cyclepath by White Cart Water. You reach this by going past Pollok House car park. It's quite pretty if you can manage to ignore the M77. Beyond this the route runs through housing estates, again near White Cart Water, which will become a familiar feature. There's a bit of footpath to use and a pelican crossing at a roundabout on Corkerhill Road but it's all clearly signposted so there should be no problem.

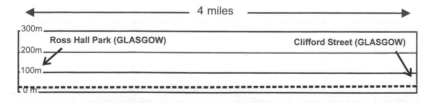

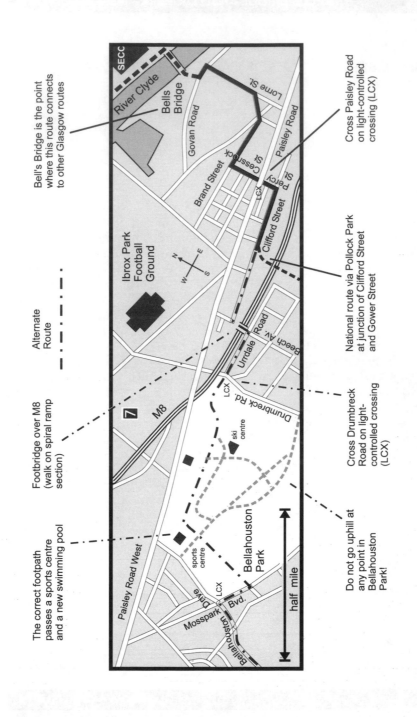

Bell's Bridge is the point where this route connects to other Glasgow routes

SECC

River Clyde

Bells Bridge

Govan Road

Brand Street

Cessnock St

Lorne St.

Paisley Road

Percy St

LCX

Clifford Street

Cross Paisley Road on light-controlled crossing (LCX)

National route via Pollock Park at junction of Clifford Street and Gower Street

Ibrox Park Football Ground

N
W E
S

Alternate Route

Footbridge over M8 (walk on spiral ramp section)

7

M8

Beech Av.

Urdale Road

Drumbreck Rd.

LCX

ski centre

Cross Drumbreck Road on light-controlled crossing (LCX)

The correct footpath passes a sports centre and a new swimming pool

sports centre

Paisley Road West

Bellahouston Park

Mosspark Bvd.

LCX

Bellahouston Drive

half mile

Do not go uphill at any point in Bellahouston Park!

ALTERNATIVE ROUTE VIA BELLAHOUSTON PARK

The route via Bellahouston Park ceased to be part of the National Cycle Network fairly recently, however I have retained it in the book as an alternative way to go. It is still signposted as a local cycle route and if you are wanting a circular bike ride, mostly in public parks, you could go out by Bellahouston Park and return via Pollok Park (the map on page 18 gives an overall view).

The junction of Clifford Street and Gower Street (Bell's Bridge end) is where the route divides to give you the choice of going by Pollok Park or Bellahouston Park. Bellahouston Park has a swimming pool, while Pollok Park has The Burrell Collection (art gallery). This choice of route offers the opportunity to create a short circular route within Glasgow taking in Ross Hall Park, Bellahouston Park and Pollok Park.

When passing through Bellahouston Park bear in mind that the cycle route through here is completely flat – if you find yourself going up or down a hill you've taken a wrong turning!

When the 1938 Empire Exhibition was held in Bellahouston Park, 13,500,000 people visited it. The centrepiece was a 300-foot-high tower built on the top of 170-foot-high Bellahouston Hill. Not a trace of all this remains nowadays. At one time Bellahouston Park also had the biggest amusment park in Europe. Nowadays there is an excellent modern swimming pool and a sports centre so plenty is still going on here. The swimming pool has a restaurant.

South-east of Bellahouston Park the route takes to quiet streets with pelican crossings to avoid road junctions (map next page). The routes merge again at a bridge over White Cart Water in Ross Hall Park, near the new Ross Hall High School. Ross Hall Park is small compared to Pollok and Bellahouston, but quite attractive with the river running through it.

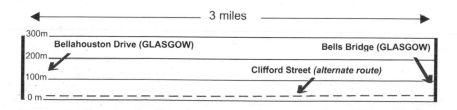

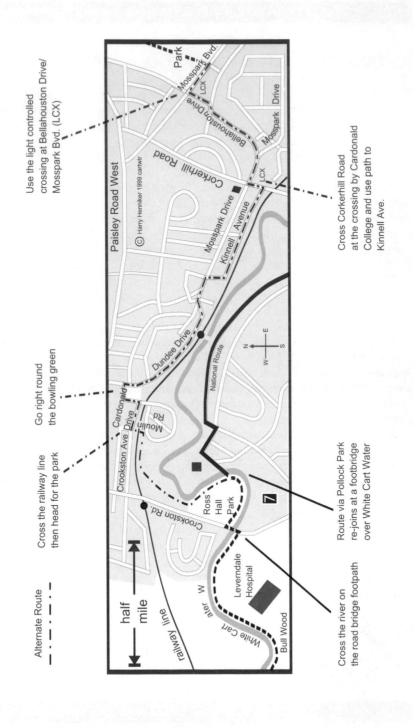

Alternate Route — · · —

Use the light controlled
crossing at Bellahouston Drive/
Mosspark Bvd. (LCX)

Cross Corkerhill Road
at the crossing by Cardonald
College and use path to
Kinnell Ave.

Go right round
the bowling green

Cross the railway line
then head for the park

Route via Pollock Park
re-joins at a footbridge
over White Cart Water

Cross the river on
the road bridge footpath

half
mile

railway line

Paisley Road West

© Harry Henniker 1999 cartwtr

Corkerhill Road

Mosspark Bvd.

LCX

Bellahouston Drive

LCX

Mosspark Drive

Park

Mosspark Drive

Kinnell Avenue

LCX

Dundee Drive

National Route

Cardonald Drive

Crookston Ave

Moulin Rd

Crookston Rd.

Ross Hall Park

7

Leverndale Hospital

White Cart Water

Bull Wood

N
W   E
S

BELLAHOUSTON PARK TO BULL WOOD
(PARTLY ALTERNATE ROUTE)

This is an area of suburban housing which should have very little traffic except where you have to cross busy roads using pelican crossings. Again the route is well signposted so you should have little problem.

Between Mosspark Boulevard and Ross Hall Park there's not much reason to stop unless you want to buy an ice cream or a drink at one of the small shops you occasionally pass. There will be a slight delay at the pelican crossing complex near Cardonald College (take care, as children may be crossing the road).

As you go along Dundee Drive near the railway there's a small rise then a descent. West of this you go round a bowling green, and just west of this again, the crossing between Cardonald Drive and Ross Hall Park is via a footbridge.

There's a children's swing in Ross Hall Park, a wood and some good places to picnic by the river.

The junction between the National Route via Pollok and the alternate route via Bellahouston is here – a small footbridge over the river, which is near a nursery school.

West of Ross Hall Park the National Route follows a path by White Cart Water again, skirting Leverndale Hospital. You have to cross Crookston Road to get between these two places and in doing so you also cross to the other river bank – use the east footpath to cross the river then go under Crookston Road using the pedestrian tunnel.

A possible diversion from here is to Crookston Castle (fifteenth century), which has connections with Mary Queen of Scots via Lord Darnley. To reach this go south down Crookston Road then turn left to Brockburn (half a mile).

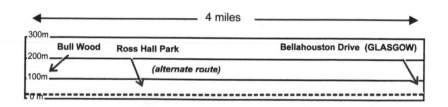

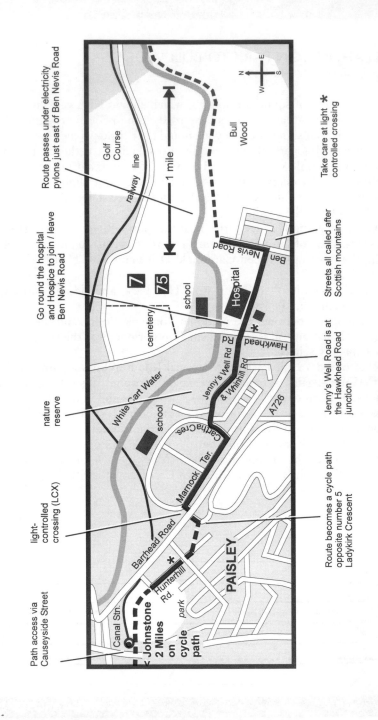

BULL WOOD TO PAISLEY CANAL STATION

Going west the cycle route runs along by White Cart Water for a time then passes by a housing estate where all the roads are called after Scottish mountains. You pass a hospice and Hawkhead Hospital and are then in urban Paisley. Take care crossing Hawkhead Road; there is a pelican crossing on Barrhead Road. The last section to Paisley Canal Station is by a public park.

The station building has now been converted into a pub with a beer garden – this might be a useful refreshment stop, or alternatively you could picnic in the park.

You are now in the centre of Paisley. Christian Paisley was founded in AD 560 by the Irish monk Mirrin, who built a small church on the bank of the Cart Water. He is buried close by and was later made into a saint – hence the name of the local football team: St Mirren.

For many people Paisley means Paisley pattern, a decorative style used on clothing and duvet covers. Paisley was also once famous for thread production but this too is now gone. What is left is a proliferation of churches. Most of these are very attractive but many are now used for non-religious purposes.

To find out about the history of Paisley the place to go is Paisley Museum and Art Gallery. Also interesting is the twelfth-century abbey which survived being set on fire by Edward I and his army in 1307 and again in 1498. Due to this the central tower collapsed but, undaunted, the monks restored it. The last restoration was in 1897 by Sir Robert Lorimer and this has produced a beautiful church. The abbey is just north of the station, a short walk along Gordon Street then Bridge Street. Paisley Arts Centre is just across the river from the Abbey and tourist information is next door.

After Paisley Canal Station the route takes to the former railway line and cycling on streets is over apart from a very short section in Elderslie.

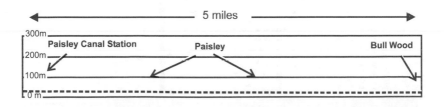

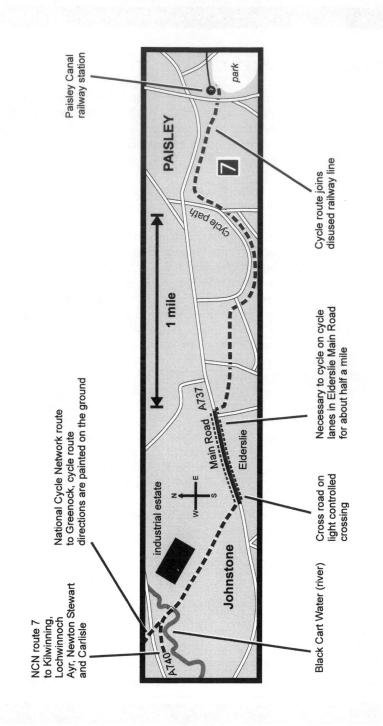

Paisley Canal railway station

Cycle route joins disused railway line

PAISLEY

cycle path

1 mile

Main Road A737

Elderslie

Necessary to cycle on cycle lanes in Elderslie Main Road for about half a mile

Cross road on light controlled crossing

industrial estate

N
W E
S

Johnstone

A740

Black Cart Water (river)

NCN route 7 to Kilwinning, Lochwinnoch Ayr, Newton Stewart and Carlisle

National Cycle Network route to Greenock, cycle route directions are painted on the ground

park

PAISLEY TO JOHNSTONE

Route-finding is easy now as it's simply a matter of following the railway path until you get to Elderslie. Here there's a brief section on road of about half a mile but it's well signposted. Bike lanes are marked; going west you cross to the right-hand side of the road on a light-controlled crossing then continue in the same direction to leave the road under a railway arch to open country.

Following this it's railway path again, passing an industrial estate. You see a weir and cross the Black Cart Water just for a change. Just west of this is the cyclepath junction offering routes to Greenock and Lochwinnoch, leading eventually to Irvine / Ardrossan / Carlisle. Last time I was there directions were painted on the ground but Sustrans may have put something fancier up by now. The route to Greenock crosses over the A740.

Elderslie, formerly known as Ellersly, was once a quiet village, but is now just a part of Paisley and Johnstone. There's evidence of a settlement going back to Bronze Age times, over 2000 years ago. There is a memorial to William Wallace near the cycle route road section in Elderslie. This is at the site of the former castle owned by the Wallaces of Ellersly. William Wallace was a son of this family who defeated the English near Stirling in 1297. Unfortunately he ended up with his head nailed to London Bridge 12 years later.

You may notice a number of street names hereabouts with the suffix 'canal'. This refers to the Glasgow–Ardrossan Canal. It was only ever finished as far as Johnstone due to lack of funds, but it was quite successful for a time – until the advent of the railways which caused it to be closed in 1882. The canal bed was converted to a railway which became the Paisley to Kilmacolm Railway, until this too was eventually closed. This is what you are cycling along.

Johnstone has been in existence for a long time as it was the only crossing place of the Black Cart Water between it and the River Clyde. It shares the weaving and thread-making history of Paisley and has now seen some regeneration in the industrial estate you passed.

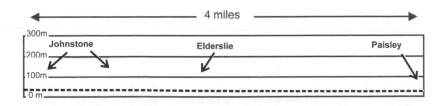

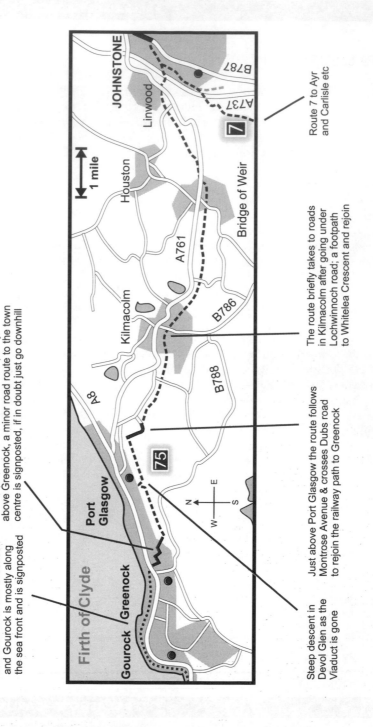

Firth of Clyde

JOHNSTONE

Linwood

Houston

1 mile

Kilmacolm

A761

A8

Port
Glasgow

B786

Gourock / Greenock

B788

Bridge of Weir

B787

A737

7

75

N
W — E
S

The route between Greenock and Gourock is mostly along the sea front and is signposted

The cycle path bike route ends in a park just above Greenock, a minor road route to the town centre is signposted, if in doubt just go downhill

The route briefly takes to roads in Kilmacolm after going under Lochwinnoch road; a footpath to Whitelea Crescent and rejoin

Route 7 to Ayr and Carlisle etc

Just above Port Glasgow the route follows Montrose Avenue & crosses Dubs road to rejoin the railway path to Greenock

Steep descent in Devol Glen as the Viaduct is gone

JOHNSTONE TO GOUROCK
(PART OF ROUTE 75, CLYDE TO FORTH ROUTE IN SUSTRANS LABELLING)

In fact the dedicated cycle route runs out at Greenock; beyond Greenock, to Gourock, the route is signposted by the sea, mostly following the sea front.

Between Greenock and Johnstone, though, it's virtually all dedicated cycle route along a former railway line. From the junction near Johnstone the path runs straight through Bridge of Weir without touching any roads. You'll find refreshment stops and food shops quite near in Bridge of Weir even if you do have to leave the cyclepath.

In Kilmacolm the continuity of the cyclepath is broken by a mock-Tudor housing estate. It's signposted through but this is a good place to stop anyway if it's lunchtime as the former railway station, now the Pullman Pub, can provide bar lunches. Kilmacolm, like Bridge of Weir, was a tiny hamlet until the railway came. It became popular with wealthy commuters working in Glasgow and there are some beautiful houses, noteably Windyhill designed by Charles Rennie Macintosh.

The continuity of the railway path is broken again just above Port Glasgow and you have to follow Montrose Avenue for half a mile (see map).

After this the path runs high above the Firth of Clyde. The townscapes of Port Glasgow and Greenock form the foreground, the green beauty of the Kyles of Bute stretches away into the distance. Just before you get to Greenock there is a steep descent into Devol Glen. The railway was carried over the glen by a viaduct. This was blown up by the army when the railway closed in 1966.

The path runs out in Greenock. You can return to Glasgow by train or cycle on to Gourock by the sea. Catching a ferry to Dunoon and cycling on Bute would also be a great idea. Greenock has a very old past – pottery from 1000 BC has been found there. It was a sugar-refining centre and made ocean liners; now IBM PCs are made there. Tracks above Greenock, around Loch Thom, are worth exploring on a mountain bike (Clyde Muirshiel Regional Park).

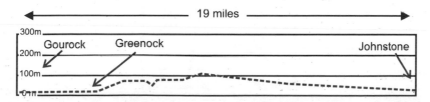

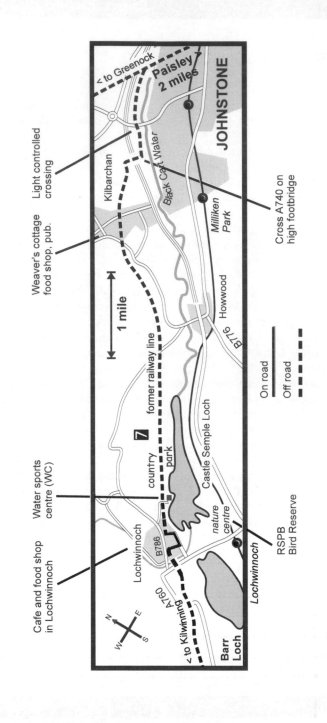

Cafe and food shop in Lochwinnoch

Water sports centre (WC)

Weaver's cottage food shop, pub.

Light controlled crossing

< to Greenock

Paisley 2 miles

JOHNSTONE

Kilbarchan

Black Cart Water

Milliken Park

Cross A740 on high footbridge

Howwood

B776

1 mile

former railway line

country park

Castle Semple Loch

On road

Off road

Lochwinnoch

B786

nature centre

RSPB Bird Reserve

A760

N
W   E
S

< to Kilwinning

Lochwinnoch

Barr Loch

JOHNSTONE TO BARR LOCH

The long-distance route to Carlisle continues south via Barr Loch. After Johnstone the route becomes increasingly rural and attractive and continues on former railway line as far as Glengarnock.

The northern part is between the A737 Johnstone bypass and the river, Black Cart Water. Going south, cross Barrochan Road on a light-controlled crossing, then shortly after turn right over the dual carriageway on a high footbridge.

After this the railway path winds past dairy farms, through attractive hilly country. Because it's a converted railway line all the hills on the route itself are very gentle.

The route runs through Kilbarchan, once an eighteenth-century weaving village where the houses were both homes and weaving shops. One of these has now been taken over by the National Trust for Scotland and completely restored to how it would have looked 200 years ago. The loom is now in working order and weaving demonstrations are given.

There is a gradual climb, then a gentle descent to Castle Semple Loch. This is popular for sailing and sculling. The watersports centre has toilets and an information display. There is a tea room. There is also a tea room in Lochwinnoch village, which is just off the route.

The whole area between Lochwinnoch and Cloch Point on the coast is now a Regional Park with nature trails, bird sanctuaries, rivers and lochs. Part of this, the nature reserve on the other side of Castle Semple Loch (see map) is in easy reach of the cycle route. This is run by the Royal Society for the Protection of Birds (RSPB). There is an observation tower, nature trail and birdwatching hides.

After the watersports centre, the route briefly follows an access road then turns right into a public park. Continue on past the children's swing park and bear left on to the railway path again. There is another gradual climb, with lots of water channels which ensure that the burns crossing the path at this point don't flood it. Barr Loch is over to the east, but it's obscured by trees.

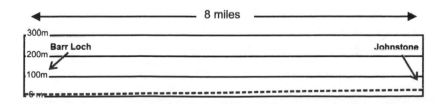

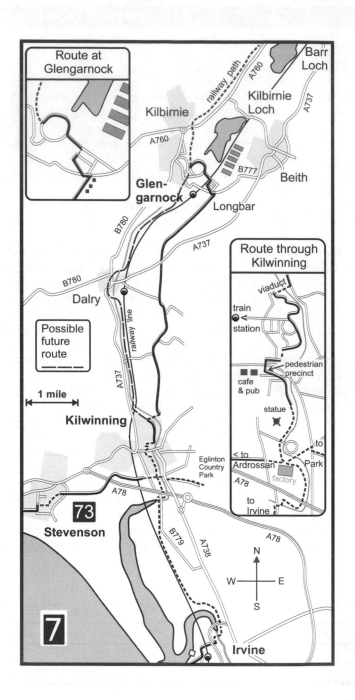

Route at Glengarnock

Barr Loch

railway path

A760

Kilbirnie Loch

A737

Kilbirnie

A760

B777

Beith

Glen-garnock

Longbar

B780

A737

B780

Dalry

railway line

Possible future route

_ _ _ _

1 mile

A737

Kilwinning

Route through Kilwinning

viaduct

train station

pedestrian precinct

cafe & pub

statue

to Park

< to Ardrossan

factory

A78

to Irvine

Eglinton Country Park

A78

73

Stevenson

B779

A738

A78

N

W — E

S

7

Irvine

BARR LOCH TO IRVINE

From Barr Loch it's former railway line to Glengarnock and after that you're on back roads again. You don't seem to be able to rely on the signs here as they tend to get stolen, so pay attention!

Southbound description: follow Caledonian Road when the cyclepath ends in a wide circle to the north. Kilbirnie Loch comes into view, together with a lot of huge industrial buildings. Cross a railway line, but look for a bike path leading off to the right. Go down this into a housing estate, going left, right and left (see map insert). Turn right off the B777, on to a minor road by three modern bungalows; climb up a steep hill. Northbound it's a left on to the B777 then of course right into the housing estate.

The route between Glengarnock and Kilwinning runs high above the village of Dalry. This section is hilly, which can be a shock after rolling easily along the railway path. The mountains of Arran can be seen, poking above the lower hills of the mainland. Just north of Kilwinning you cross a railway viaduct near a housing estate.

To get through the estate follow the River Garnock (see map insert). At the south end this comes out at the A737 by the river. Just beyond this is the pedestrian precinct in the town (walk). There is a good Italian restaurant and a pub, plus the usual shops. Eglinton Country Park is quite near.

There is a park just south of Kilwinning and the cyclepath runs through this by the River Garnock. Just south of a statue in the park the route splits into two with a spur (National Cycle Route 73) leading off to Ardrossan (handy for the ferry to Arran), if you're not going to Ardrossan it's just a matter of keeping straight on.

Just south of this junction the route passes under the A78, then briefly takes to the B779 to cross the river. After that it's dedicated cyclepath again all the way to Irvine. Going through Irvine itself the route takes to streets after crossing the river and the A737. Again stay by the river and you'll pick up the cyclepath again near the Magnum Leisure Centre.

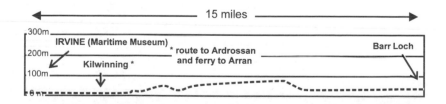

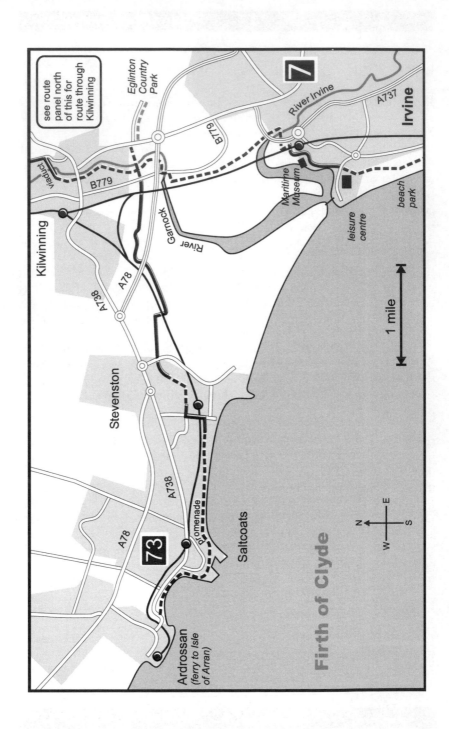

see route panel north of this for route through Kilwinning

Eglinton Country Park

7

River Irvine

A737

Irvine

B779

Viaduct

B779

Kilwinning

River Garnock

Maritime Museum

beach park

leisure centre

A738

A78

Stevenston

1 mile

A738

A78

73

promenade

Saltcoats

Ardrossan
(ferry to Isle of Arran)

Firth of Clyde

N
E
W
S

KILWINNING TO ARDROSSAN (NCN ROUTE 73)

This section isn't particularly attractive but can be very useful as a way to get to the ferry for Arran.

Leave the pedestrian precinct in Kilwinning by biking east towards the river, then follow the signposted bike route by the river bank. Enter Alumswell Park, pass a circular statue on the right, ignore the first steel footbridge over the river, but turn right, away from the river, in front of a white factory building by the second bridge. Continuing straight on takes you to Irvine and turning left over the river takes you to Eglinton Country Park.

Now travelling west, leave Alumswell Park, cross a road and follow a minor road running parallel to the A78 dual carriageway. Pass under a railway then under the A78. After a mile cross the B752 and enter Ardeer Park, cycling by a golf course. You emerge at Moorpark Road East. Turn left, over a railway level crossing and immediately turn right. This becomes a footpath by sand dunes. Pass a caravan park and follow the promenade through Saltcoats to Ardrossan.

The name Saltcoats simply means 'saltworkers cottages' and this was the initial reason for the development of the town. Later it became a popular holiday resort, reached by rail from Glasgow, though the advent of the foreign package holiday ended all that.

Nowadays the only ferry sailing from Ardrossan is the one going to Arran, but at one time ferries sailed from here to Ireland and the Isle of Man. The harbour was even at one time a transatlantic port.

Arran is certainly the most popular island in Scotland for cycling – the ferry often carries more bicycles than cars and the roads are relatively quiet, particularly on the west coast. Arran is hilly but very scenic. Fit cyclists could cycle most of the roads in a weekend, but if that wasn't enough you could catch a ferry over to Claonaig on the Mull of Kintyre (summer only) and continue there. The Cycle Network is being extended to cover this area – see the map at the beginning of the book. This will mostly consist of road signs so there isn't any reason not to do it immediately if that's your desire. This book, however, describes routes in mainland Scotland.

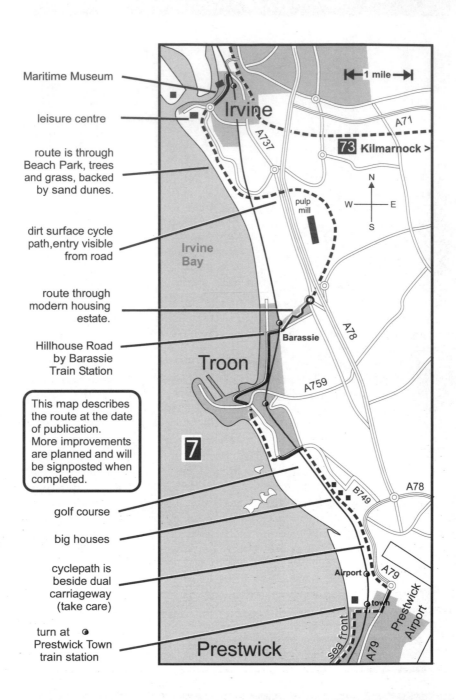

Maritime Museum

leisure centre

route is through Beach Park, trees and grass, backed by sand dunes.

dirt surface cycle path, entry visible from road

route through modern housing estate.

Hillhouse Road by Barassie Train Station

This map describes the route at the date of publication. More improvements are planned and will be signposted when completed.

golf course

big houses

cyclepath is beside dual carriageway (take care)

turn at ● Prestwick Town train station

Irvine

Maritime Museum

A71

73 Kilmarnock >

A737

N
W—E
S

pulp mill

Irvine Bay

Barassie

A78

Troon

A759

7

B749

A78

Airport ○ ○ A79

○ town

Prestwick Airport

Sea front

A79

Prestwick

1 mile

IRVINE TO PRESTWICK

While this section is interesting and at times scenic, there are some places where improvements are still needed to bring the route up to standard. Around Prestwick Airport you seem to be surrounded by heavy trains on one side, while on the other jumbo jets and articulated lorries thunder by. In fact, it's relatively safe as you are on a cyclepath beside the A79. Never mind, the peace and quiet of South Ayrshire is quite near.

There's plenty to do in Irvine, what with the Maritime Museum and Magnum Leisure Centre. If all that isn't your scene you might like to visit the Glasgow Vennel. This is a street which was the main road to Glasgow in the fifteenth century. It's been restored and gives a unique feel of what it was really like several centuries ago. Robert Burns came to live and work here in 1781. You can find out more about all this in the Glasgow Vennel Museum.

Troon is an attractive town famous for its golf course, the Royal Troon, founded in 1878. There are tea rooms and pubs and lots of Edwardian and Victorian houses as well as modern mansions. The beaches are quiet. There are four other golf courses apart from the Royal Troon.

One good thing about this section is that there are plenty of train stations – if the weather turns bad, or if you just want a day trip it's quite easy to hop on a train with your bike to return to Glasgow or wherever.

Prestwick isn't quite as attractive as Troon but there should be good views towards Arran as you cycle along the sea front. Unfortunately you have to do a little bit beside the A79 near Prestwick Airport. To get between the A79 and the sea front you use a back road running by Prestwick Town railway station. There are bike shops in Prestwick, Troon and Irvine as well as all the usual facilities.

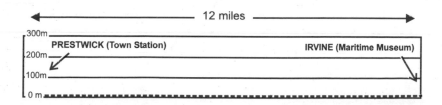

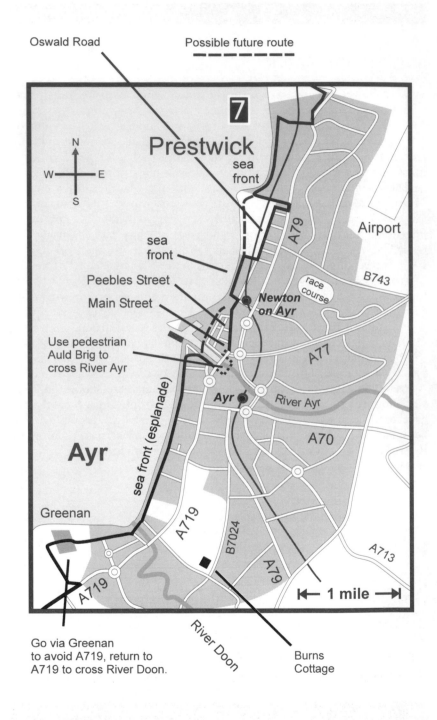

Oswald Road

Possible future route

Prestwick

7

sea front

Airport

A79

B743

sea front

race course

Peebles Street

Newton on Ayr

Main Street

Use pedestrian Auld Brig to cross River Ayr

A77

Ayr

River Ayr

sea front (esplanade)

A70

Ayr

Greenan

A719

B7024

A79

A713

1 mile

Go via Greenan to avoid A719, return to A719 to cross River Doon.

River Doon

Burns Cottage

PRESTWICK TO AYR

AYR, A TOUN THAT NONE SURPASSES,
FOR HONEST LADS AND BONNIE LASSIES.

Sitting in a café in Ayr, having just cycled from Maybole, I reflected that this piece of doggerel by Burns still seemed to be true – Ayr is still full of bonnie lassies. Mind you, I can't vouch for the honest lads, perhaps you'd be as well to lock your bike up anyway.

The cycle route south of Ayr is quite straightforward, but from north of Ayr to Prestwick it was a bit of a mess when I went through, although I was struggling to find cyclepaths which didn't at that time exist. If you stick to the roads indicated you shouldn't have problems. If an improved route is in place you can rely on it being signposted.

Ayr grew up around a castle which was destroyed by Robert the Bruce in 1298 to keep it from English hands. The racecourse is famous and the harbour is worth walking round in the evening after your bike ride. There are plenty of good pubs and places to eat and you should have no trouble finding a B&B if you're staying over.

The tourist industry in Ayr is of course centred on Robert Burns. The Auld Brig o' Doon (near Burns Cottage), featured in 'Tam o' Shanter' is now so renovated and surrounded by flower beds that it hardly seems 'Auld' at all. Tam, if you remember, fled from the witch Cutty Sark and was saved when he crossed the bridge as witches cannot cross running water. The incident is commemorated in the clipper ship of that name, now preserved in Greenwich in London.

Burns Cottage is well worth visiting however, and the associated museum is fascinating to anyone who enjoys Burns's poetry or song. The nearby Tam o' Shanter Experience should be fun for children.

There's a lot more to Ayr than Robert Burns, of course: Queens Court shopping Arcade is a lovely restoration and there's two miles of beach with a great view of Ailsa Craig and Arran. While the cycle route is mostly fine, the town isn't very suitable for cycling, so it would probably be better to walk round if you want to explore.

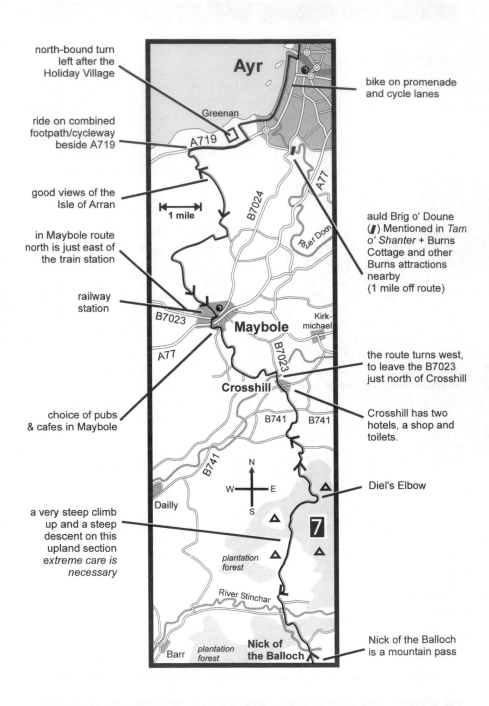

north-bound turn left after the Holiday Village

bike on promenade and cycle lanes

ride on combined footpath/cycleway beside A719

good views of the Isle of Arran

1 mile

Ayr

Greenan

A719

B7024

A77

River Doon

auld Brig o' Doune (⚑) Mentioned in *Tam o' Shanter* + Burns Cottage and other Burns attractions nearby (1 mile off route)

in Maybole route north is just east of the train station

railway station

B7023

A77

Maybole

Kirk-michael

B7023

the route turns west, to leave the B7023 just north of Crosshill

choice of pubs & cafes in Maybole

Crosshill

B741

B741

Crosshill has two hotels, a shop and toilets.

a very steep climb up and a steep descent on this upland section *extreme care is necessary*

B741

Dailly

N
W — E
S

Diel's Elbow

7

plantation forest

River Stinchar

Barr

plantation forest

Nick of the Balloch

Nick of the Balloch is a mountain pass

AYR TO NICK OF THE BALLOCH

'Nick' in this connection means mountain pass. You could argue, I suppose, that the hills of South Ayrshire aren't really mountains, but there are certainly some of the steepest hills I've ever encountered on a bike. There's nothing actually at Nick of the Balloch, except possibly a few sheep, so make sure you've got enough provisions before sailing off into the wilds of Galloway.

From Greenan just outside Ayr there's a two-mile section on a combined footpath / cycleway beside the A719. After this you turn south to a minor road which climbs Brown Carrick Hill; this marks the transition from the populated, flatter country of the Scottish central belt to the steep hills of South Ayrshire. You won't need me to tell you this if you're actually there on a bike.

There's a good view of the Isle of Arran, then several ups and downs on the high section. If you're descending to Maybole check your brakes first; if you're going up, get in to bottom gear at the foot of the hill.

Maybole has several tea rooms, quite a lot of pubs and shops and a good supermarket. Also here is the last railway station you'll encounter for some time. If you're going north, note that the railway station is next to the road on which you leave the town. Maybole grew up as a market town serving the wild hinterland of Carrick – at one time its citizens were renowned for their longevity, which was attributed to the mild, enervating climate.

Just south of Maybole the route follows the railway for a little while, crossing it twice, then the railway line shoots off to the south-west following the Water of Girvan while the cycle route retains its north–south axis, Crosshill being the last village before Glen Trool (next page).

Crosshill is an old weaving village with whitewashed houses. There are toilets, two hotels and a shop but no café. South of Crosshill the land is given over to forestry. Allow plenty of time between Glen Trool and Crosshill as the hills will slow you down, but it's a lovely remote area – take your time and enjoy it.

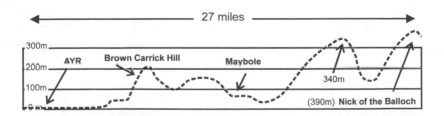

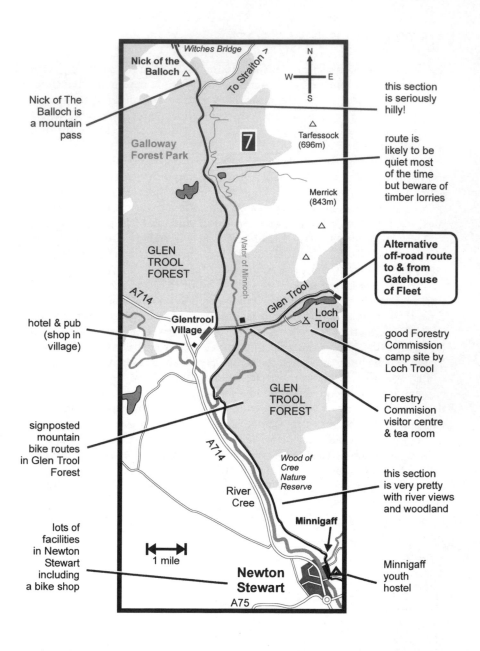

Witches Bridge

Nick of the Balloch △

To Straiton ↗

N
W ← → E
S

Nick of The Balloch is a mountain pass

Galloway Forest Park

7

△ Tarfessock (696m)

this section is seriously hilly!

route is likely to be quiet most of the time but beware of timber lorries

Merrick (843m)

△

△

GLEN TROOL FOREST

Water of Minnoch

A714

Glen Trool

Loch Trool

△

Alternative off-road route to & from Gatehouse of Fleet

Glentrool Village

hotel & pub (shop in village)

good Forestry Commission camp site by Loch Trool

GLEN TROOL FOREST

Forestry Commision visitor centre & tea room

signposted mountain bike routes in Glen Trool Forest

A714

Wood of Cree Nature Reserve

this section is very pretty with river views and woodland

River Cree

Minnigaff

lots of facilities in Newton Stewart including a bike shop

1 mile

Newton Stewart

Minnigaff youth hostel

A75

NICK OF THE BALLOCH TO NEWTON STEWART

If you are going south, once you're over the Nick, life becomes somewhat easier. Going north, you ain't seen nothing yet. Galloway Forest Park is a huge area with lots of wildlife: red deer, pine martens, wild goats, otters and wintering wildfowl from the Arctic in the 'flowes'. Much of the area is plantation forest but mixed woodland still remains. Going through in the spring, look for sheets of colourful bluebells.

Don't be under the illusion that you are cycling in a natural forest, for most of the trees have been planted by the Forestry Commission. Scotland's natural forest started disappearing around AD 800 and was mostly gone by the end of the eighteenth century. The final destruction was caused by the demand for timber during the two World Wars.

The Forestry Commission has its roots in the fact that much timber had to be convoyed across the Atlantic during the First World War. It was established in 1919 with the aim of making Britain more self-sufficient in timber. The sitka spruce is the most common tree.

Nowadays there is more emphasis on the recreational use of forest, and a wider variety of trees is being planted with more consideration being given to landscaping. Perhaps one day we will have our ancient woodlands back, with oak, Scots pine and birch ruling the hills again.

Glentrool Village is much engaged in forestry but there is some accommodation, a small shop and a hotel which does bar lunches.

The west end of the alternative off-road route to Gatehouse of Fleet is here. This is a great way to go if you like mountain biking, but don't start it late in the afternoon unless you are equipped for camping. There is a bothy (rough shelter) near Loch Dee (see next page). The forest visitor centre is one mile up Glen Trool. We enjoyed the chocolate cake in the tea room. The camp site further up the glen is excellent and has a shop.

Another place to stay around here is Minnigaff Youth Hostel which is excellent. There are lots of B&Bs in Newton Stewart. The route between Glentrool Village and Newton Stewart is really beautiful with wild flowers, oak and birch beside the river.

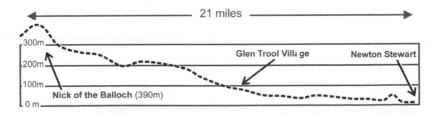

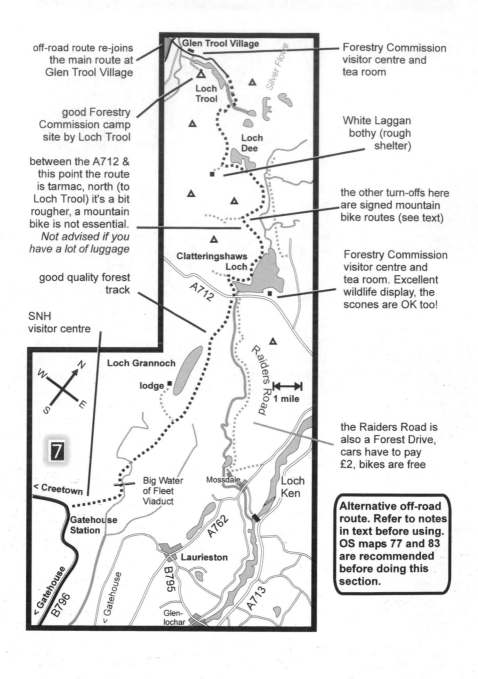

off-road route re-joins the main route at Glen Trool Village

Forestry Commission visitor centre and tea room

good Forestry Commission camp site by Loch Trool

White Laggan bothy (rough shelter)

between the A712 & this point the route is tarmac, north (to Loch Trool) it's a bit rougher, a mountain bike is not essential. *Not advised if you have a lot of luggage*

the other turn-offs here are signed mountain bike routes (see text)

good quality forest track

Forestry Commission visitor centre and tea room. Excellent wildlife display, the scones are OK too!

SNH visitor centre

the Raiders Road is also a Forest Drive, cars have to pay £2, bikes are free

Glen Trool Village

Silver Flowe

Loch Trool

Loch Dee

Loch Grannoch

lodge

Clatteringshaws Loch

A712

Raiders Road

1 mile

7

< Creetown

Big Water of Fleet Viaduct

Mossdale

Loch Ken

Gatehouse Station

A762

< Gatehouse

Gatehouse

Laurieston

B795

A713

B796

Glen-lochar

Alternative off-road route. Refer to notes in text before using. OS maps 77 and 83 are recommended before doing this section.

ALTERNATIVE OFF-ROAD ROUTE VIA GLEN TROOL

This is an alternative route avoiding Newton Stewart. If you like mountain biking this is the way to go. The route via Newton Stewart is also very attractive. You might like to purchase OS Landranger map sheets 77 and 83 before going off into the forest as the map opposite is not really adequate for navigation off-road.

This would be easier on a mountain bike but it would be possible to do it on any bike, though it would be hard work if you had a lot of luggage. There are numerous spots where it would be possible to camp. If there has been recent rain parts of the route could be muddy. You could be a long way from help, so a spare inner tube and a chain tool is a good idea.

From Glentrool Village the road climbs gently at first then steeply above Loch Trool. A short walk here takes you to Bruce's Stone, commemorating Robert the Bruce's first victory on the road to Scottish independence. It's worth going for the view. East of this the route becomes a steep dirt track. After passing through an oak wood the route becomes easier following forest roads.

The route to Clatteringshaws Loch has some steady ups and downs but none of them are really steep; there are good views of Loch Dee and the Silver Flowe. If you are needing somewhere to sleep, White Laggan Bothy (see map) might be suitable but you would need a sleeping bag. The section by Clatteringshaws Loch has a tarmac surface. The visitor centre at Clatteringshaws Loch is a mile off the route on the relatively quiet A712. There are some excellent wildlife displays and a good tea room.

South of Clatteringshaws the route now goes by Loch Grannoch and the Big Water of Fleet viaduct. This is all forest road again. The Big Water of Fleet Viaduct is a disused railway viaduct – the cycle route doesn't actually run along it. Just south of this again is a Scottish Natural Heritage visitor centre which is interesting. The off-road route meets the B796 six miles north of Gatehouse of Fleet at Gatehouse Station. At this point you rejoin the main National Cycle Network route which has gone via Minnigaff (Newton Stewart).

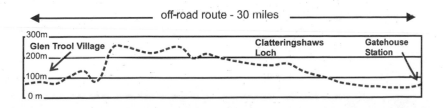

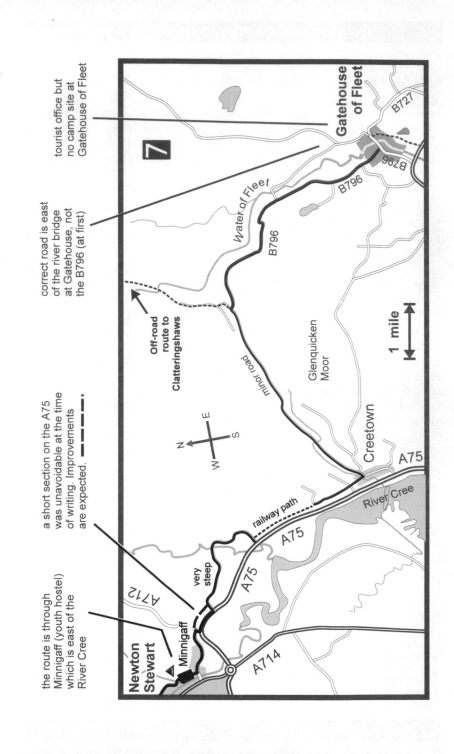

the route is through
Minnigaff (youth hostel)
which is east of the
River Cree

a short section on the A75
was unavoidable at the time
of writing. Improvements
are expected. ▬ ▬ ▬

correct road is east
of the river bridge
at Gatehouse, not
the B796 (at first)

tourist office but
no camp site at
Gatehouse of Fleet

7

Gatehouse
of Fleet

B727

B796

Water of Fleet

B796

B796

Off-road
route to
Clatteringshaws

minor road

Glenquicken
Moor

1 mile

N
W — E
S

Creetown

A75

railway path

River Cree

A75

A75

very
steep

A712

Newton
Stewart

Minnigaff

A714

NEWTON STEWART TO GATEHOUSE OF FLEET

Like most Galloway towns Newton Stewart isn't particularly touristy but it has all the necessary facilities, including a bike shop. There is an excellent youth hostel in a former school over the river in Minnigaff.

Newton Stewart was founded in 1677 by William Stewart of nearby Castle Stewart. The town grew rapidly – a local minister writing in 1793 said that its growth had been simply amazing. At that time the then owner of the town, local landowner William Douglas, tried to change the name to Newton Douglas but local opposition prevented this.

At the time of writing, south of Newton Stewart there is a short section on the A75. Take care if this has not been improved. After this the route goes past Kirroughtree Forest which has some marked mountain bike routes and a visitor centre with a tea room.

Creetown is noteable for its Gem Rock Museum. I'm not particularly interested in precious stones, but I was down there with a group of cyclists a couple of years ago and it was a rainy day so we went in – I was quite impressed. There's a camp site in Creetown and a pub, shop and café.

The route over Glenquicken moor is a steady climb but has fine views and it's a fast descent through woods (or a stiff climb in the other direction) to Gatehouse of Fleet.

Gatehouse (nobody bothers with the rest) is a pretty town with colour-washed buildings at the head of the Fleet estuary. It doesn't look like it now, but there was a thriving cotton-spinning and weaving business here in the eighteenth century. You can still visit the water mill which has displays and a restaurant. They also do quite an impressive slide show about local history and wildlife. There isn't any camp site or youth hostel, but the local tourist office will find you a B&B easily enough.

At one time there were four water mills in Gatehouse and the supply of water power for the mills became inadequate. A 6.4km water course was constructed to improve this, and eventually became useful for transport. It ended at nearby Skyreburn Bay and this termination still survives, being used for pleasure craft.

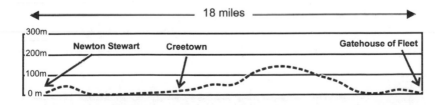

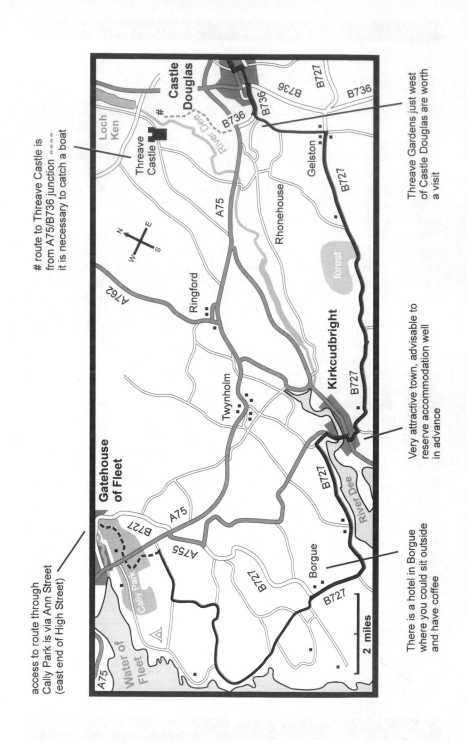

access to route through
Cally Park is via Ann Street
(east end of High Street)

route to Threave Castle is
from A75/B736 junction -----
it is necessary to catch a boat

Threave Gardens just west
of Castle Douglas are worth
a visit

Very attractive town, advisable to
reserve accommodation well
in advance

There is a hotel in Borgue
where you could sit outside
and have coffee

2 miles

GATEHOUSE OF FLEET TO CASTLE DOUGLAS

From Gatehouse, the route goes through Cally Park which is situated at the south-east edge of the town. Go down the High Street travelling east and turn right down Ann Street. The adjacent plant nursery is worth a visit (it is in the walled garden). The route is signposted through the park. It takes you under the A75 to a minor road where you turn right. After this the route runs near the coast for a while and there are views across Wigtown Bay. After ten miles you join the B727 at Borgue which takes you on to Kirkcudbright via the Dee Estuary. The spit of land you see before you enter Kirkcudbright is St Mary's Isle.

Kirkcudbright is an attractive fishing port. Still the haunt of artists, it has a historic old high street with pastel-painted Scottish townhouses. The harbour is still a working fishing centre – a fleet of scallop boats are based here and they were landing fish when we cycled through. There is a wide choice of places to eat or alternatively you could picnic in the park by the harbour. The Tolbooth Art Centre is the place to go if you are interested in the town's art history. A large number of artists and craftworkers are still working in Kirkcudbright.

Between Kirkcudbright and Castle Douglas the route is mostly on the B727. From Gelston (no facilities) the route runs north–south on a minor road which ends at Carlingwark Loch. On the opposite side of the road here are Threave Gardens. These are run by the National Trust for Scotland, students from the associated horticultural school have worked magic on the place. Threave Castle is quite near too; you have to get to it on a boat, access is from the A75 (see map). You enter Castle Douglas by the B736.

Castle Douglas itself has a choice of cafés ranging from the greasy spoon variety to more upmarket ones and there's a bike shop and a tourist office. The one-time owner of the town, William Douglas (who also owned Newton Stewart, see earlier) was ultimately successful in getting his name adopted for the town here; it was previously called Carlingwark. Castle Douglas was developed by William Douglas so one imagines his preferences had greater force than at Newton Stewart.

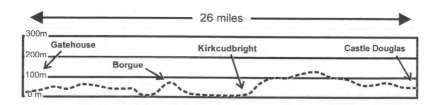

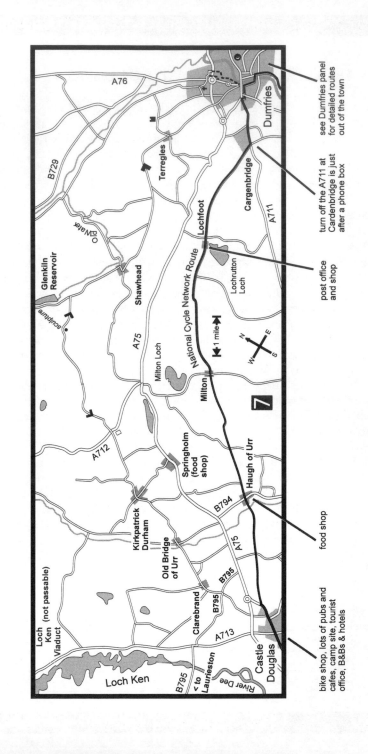

A76

B729

Old Water

Glenkiln Reservoir

sculpture

Shawhead

A75

Milton Loch

Terregles

Lochfoot

Cargenbridge

A711

Lochrutton Loch

National Cycle Network Route

1 mile

N
W — E
S

Milton

7

Haugh of Urr

Springholm (food shop)

A712

B794

Kirkpatrick Durham

A75

Old Bridge of Urr

B795

Clarebrand

B795

A713

Castle Douglas

A713

River Dee

< to Laurieston

B795

Loch Ken

Loch Ken Viaduct (not passable)

Dumfries

see Dumfries panel for detailed routes out of the town

turn off the A711 at Cardenbridge is just after a phone box

post office and shop

food shop

bike shop, lots of pubs and cafes, camp site, tourist office, B&Bs & hotels

CASTLE DOUGLAS TO DUMFRIES
AND LAURIESTON TO DUMFRIES ALTERNATIVE

The National Cycle Network route is shown on the map, as usual in red. Once it was envisaged that the route would run further north and this is still reflected in the map as a northern (circular?) option.

The National Route goes by Haugh of Urr, Milton and Lochfoot. This is attractive with fine open views. There are some sections with thorn hedges. This is not usually a problem as the thorns are normally firmly attached to the hedge. However, when we cycled over it the hedges were being trimmed and the road was strewn with cuttings. Even tyres with puncture-resistant Kevlar linings are certain to be punctured by thorns, so if you see a tractor ahead and trimmings on the road, don't blithely cycle through them.

Dumfries, like the other towns in the region, has retained the intimate size and character of a small market town. Dumfries is largely red sandstone, with handsome Victorian and Georgian buildings set in tidy streets. The broad River Nith runs through with bridges of every size and age crossing it. It was a settlement in Roman times due to its strategic position on a river crossing. The marsh to the east, Lochar Moss, probably saved the town from the worst effects of the wars with England.

Tobias Smollett, writing in 1771, said: 'A very elegant trading town . . . where we found plenty of good provisions and excellent wine, at very reasonable prices, and accommodation as good in all respects as in any part of South Britain. If I was confined to Scotland for life, I would choose Dumfries as my place of residence.' You won't have any problems finding food or drink either, there's a bike shop too nowadays, and a railway station.

A building worth looking at in Dumfries is the town house, Mid Steeple, which is in the centre of the high street. Constructed in 1707, it was felt that: 'The town is not at present provided with sufficient prisons, whereby several malefactors guilty of great crimes have made their escape to the dishonour and imminent peril of the burgh.'

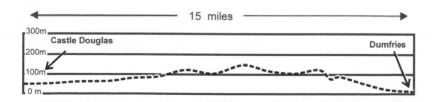

ROUTES THROUGH DUMFRIES

NATIONAL CYCLE NETWORK TO GATEHOUSE OF FLEET
GOING WEST: From the tourist office in Whitesands look south across the river and you'll see a suspension footbridge – cross the river on that. After this go upstream passing a fallow deer park. Just before the main road crosses the river, turn left into Maxwell Street. Cross the A710 / New Abbey Road to Corberry Avenue then turn right into Hermitage Drive. Turn left into Dalbeattie Road / A711 and after a mile, in Cargenbridge, shortly after a phone box, turn right on to a minor road for Lochfoot. (Note: this is an interim route.)

GOING EAST: Follow the above instructions in reverse, reading left for right of course; note that entry to Hermitage Drive is a right turn just before the A780 / A711 junction.

ALTERNATIVE ROUTE TO GATEHOUSE (NOT NCN AND NOT SIGNPOSTED)
GOING WEST: From the tourist office in Whitesands continue upstream by the river to the swimming pool just upstream of the bridge carrying the main road over the river (Buccleugh Street). Cross the river on a footbridge just north of the swimming pool. From here it's signposted as a cycle route by the local council: 'K.M. Trail'. Follow this across the A75 to Lochside on to Hardthorn Road, left at castle, right in Terregles to a minor road.

GOING EAST: From Terregles follow the above instructions in reverse. Note that from Hardthorn Road you turn left into Alloway Road, right at a modern church, then left to cross the A76. There are two footbridges over the A75, so use the one to the east, not the big one near the roundabout which leads you onto a dual carriageway.

NATIONAL CYCLE NETWORK TO ANNAN AND CARLISLE
Between the tourist office at Whitesands and Kingholm Quay keep by the river all the way, using paths in parks where appropriate. Entry to the cyclepath is by going round the dock at Kingholm Quay. Join the B725 at the roundabout east of the quay.

Dumfries was at one time an important port and Kingholm Quay is a remnant of this. Navigation was always difficult because of shifting sandbanks and the coming of the railway killed it off.

KIRKPATRICK MACMILLAN

Just in case you didn't know, the world's first pedal-powered bicycle was created in Dumfries and Galloway by a Scottish blacksmith, Kirkpatrick Macmillan, in 1839. The pedals were connected to the rear wheel by a system of rods and cranks. Kirkpatrick Macmillan lived at Keir Mill near Drumlanrig Castle; a reproduction of the machine can be seen at the Cycle Museum there, together with a host of other bicycles covering a period of over 100 years.

Recently the local council has developed a cycle route taking in Keir Mill and Drumlanrig. It starts in Dumfries and the local tourist information office can provide a leaflet describing it – it's called, as you must have realized by now, the K.M. Trail.

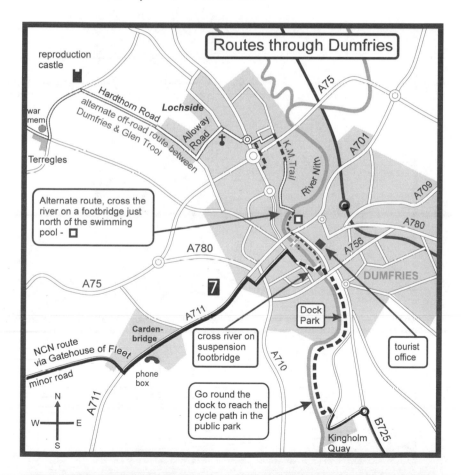

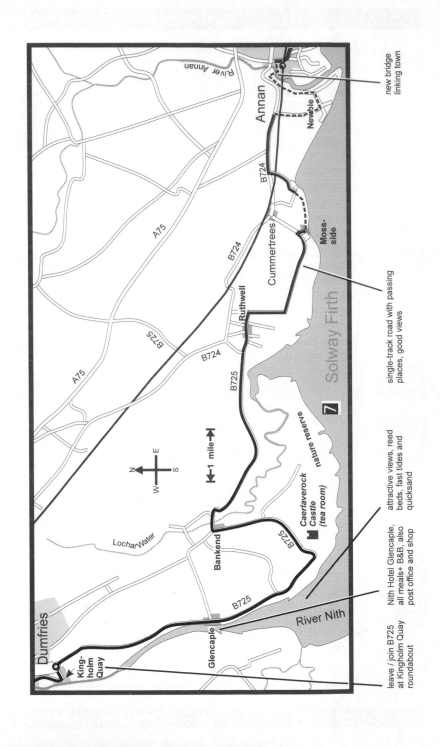

Dumfries

Kingholm Quay

River Nith

Glencaple

B725

Bankend

Caerlaverock Castle (tea room)

B725

LocharWater

nature reserve

Solway Firth

7

B725

B724

Ruthwell

B725

A75

B724

Cummertrees

Moss-side

B724

A75

Annan

River Annan

Newbie

new bridge linking town

single-track road with passing places, good views

attractive views, reed beds, fast tides and quicksand

Nith Hotel Glencaple, all meals+ B&B, also post office and shop

leave / join B725 at Kingholm Quay roundabout

N
W E
S

1 mile

DUMFRIES TO ANNAN

The western part of this section, between Dumfries and Ruthwell, uses the B725, and this is reasonably quiet with fine views over the Nith Estuary and Solway Firth. Wandering out on to the sands and mud flats can be hazardous though as there are fast tides and quicksands.

The coastline is important for wintering wildfowl from the Arctic region who take advantage of the salt-marshes and vast mudflats. Just beyond Caerlaverock Castle is Caerlaverock Wildfowl and Wetlands Centre.

There are towers and hides by several ponds for close-up views: Bewick's swans, white-fronted geese, and at least nine species of duck. In late September you might see the sky darken as thousands of barnacle geese arrive from Spitzbergen. Caerlaverock also has a population of natterjack toads.

Caerlaverock Castle is one of the most imposing castles in Scotland. Built out of red sandstone, it gives an impression of solid strength. The double tower gatehouse, triangular layout, water moat and earth ramparts give an air of impregnability, but despite all this it still fell to Edward I in 1300 in a siege conducted with ruthless efficiency.

Caerlaverock is unusual in that it is not on a hill but on flat land close to woodland swamps. It has been speculated that it may be built on the site of an old Roman harbour. The home of the Maxwell family, it was a residence as well as a stronghold. It was restored and improved by the Maxwells in the fifteenth and sixteenth centuries and there are guest chambers, carved pediments and sculptures; most of the rooms on the upper floor have windows, latrines and fireplaces. The visitor centre includes a tea room.

Between Ruthwell and Cummertrees the route takes to back roads and a coastal lane near Mossside. There are no shops in Ruthwell but the Savings Bank Museum might be of interest. There are good views of the Solway Firth and the hill of Criffel, on the far side of the Nith Estuary, from the single-track road between Ruthwell and Cummertrees. A coastal footpath was definately not OK to ride on when I was there last, though you could go as far as Newbie no problem (see map).

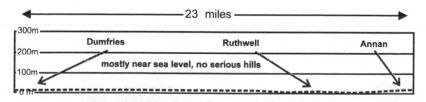

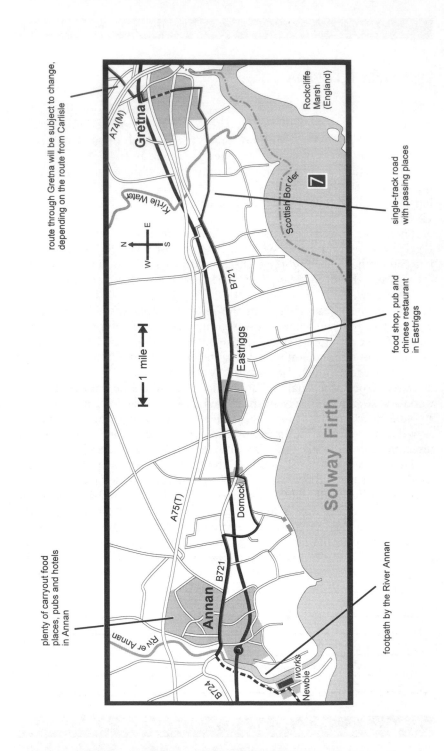

route through Gretna will be subject to change, depending on the route from Carlisle

Rockcliffe Marsh (England)

Scottish Border

[7]

single-track road with passing places

Kirtle Water

A74(M)

Gretna

N
W — E
S

B721

← 1 mile →

Eastriggs

food shop, pub and chinese restaurant in Eastriggs

Solway Firth

A75(T)

Dornock

B721

Annan

River Annan

plenty of carryout food places, pubs and hotels in Annan

B721

Newbie

works

footpath by the River Annan

ANNAN TO GRETNA GREEN

Annan, being further east and so nearer to England, suffered much more than Dumfries in the various wars between Scotland and England. In addition it was partly washed away by a flood of the River Annan in 1200. Like Dumfries it's now a solid Victorian town built of red sandstone. There's a choice of pubs, cafés and carry-outs in the main street as well as a railway station.

There was a plan to use a series of tracks by the coast east of Annan but this has been abandoned at present due to local difficulties. Because of this the route between Annan and Gretna is mostly on the B721. The B721 is reasonably quiet but what traffic there is tends to be fast.

Gretna Green is for many visitors, travelling north up the A74, their first taste of Scotland. The piper touting for tips and the coach park give it away as a tourist trap.

Gretna was of course made famous by a now-forgotten difference in the law between Scotland and England, where a declaration in front of witnesses was sufficient to formalise a marriage. Marriage in Scotland was possible at an earlier age. You can still undergo a mock ceremony in the smithy if you desire. Gretna is mostly about money, but graffiti with hearts and arrows shows that some couples are still struck by the idea of running away together and defying a heartless world.

An interesting point is that when the legislation for the new Scottish Parliament was being considered, the issues raised by Gretna were kept in mind and certain matters were retained for the UK, rather than being devolved to Scotland. Perhaps this is a lost opportunity for Gretna: issues such as the legalisation of cannabis, abortion and divorce are unlikely to offer new opportunities to exploit the legal differences between Scotland and England.

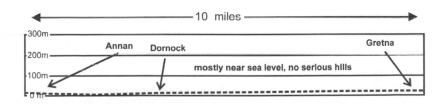

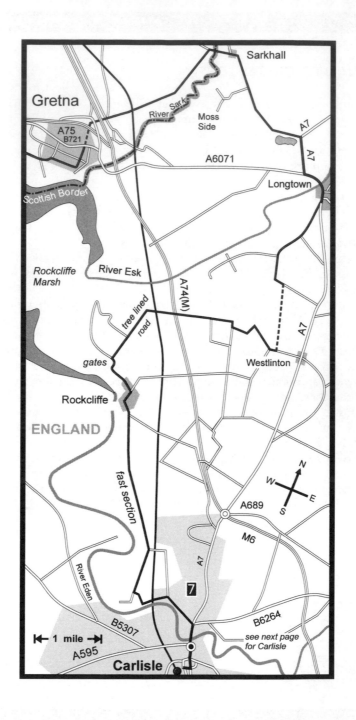

GRETNA GREEN TO CARLISLE

There are a number of routes you might use to travel between Carlisle and Gretna: the route shown opposite was finally decided in May 2000 and should be good until at least 2005. It's fairly indirect but it's the pleasure that counts not the speed. This section should be mostly fairly quiet, it's also mostly flat and quite scenic.

Gretna is of course the place where most people enter Scotland around here – driving along the motorway. You won't be doing that of course and will in fact enter or leave Scotland three miles east of Gretna near the hamlet of Sarkhall. Just south of Longtown look for a cyclepath just east of the A7 – this is both quieter and shorter.

A possible stop for a pub lunch might be at the Crown and Thistle in the village of Rockcliffe; food is also available at Longtown. The stretch of road used by the route just south of Rockcliffe is usually reasonably quiet, but what traffic there is does tend to race along as the road is quite straight – if pulling out bear in mind that cars may be travelling quickly. It is planned to eventually replace this part with a route through a nature reserve, or possibly on the old A74 when it is upgraded to motorway.

Carlisle is of course in England. It's a historic town. The list of famous people who have passed through include the Emperor Hadrian, William Wallace, Rob Roy, Robert the Bruce and Bonnie Prince Charlie. Tullie House Museum and Art Gallery has many excellent displays illustrating all this and some of the exhibits are 'hands on'. There's an interesting display of Roman relics.

Also interesting is Carlisle Castle and the cathedral; if that's not your scene the pedestrianised shopping centre has won several awards and you can't avoid it anyway as the cycle route goes right through.

Carlisle also has direct rail links to most major centres in the UK, plus the scenic Settle–Carlisle railway along which they sometimes run steam trains. Needless to say many trunk roads and the M6 motorway pass by Carlisle, but you'll be avoiding these. The National Cycle Network continues south from Carlisle to Penrith and onwards. In Penrith it joins with the C2C connecting it to Tynemouth, but all that is outside the scope of this particular book.

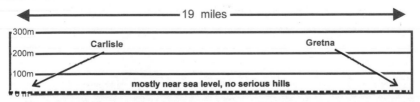

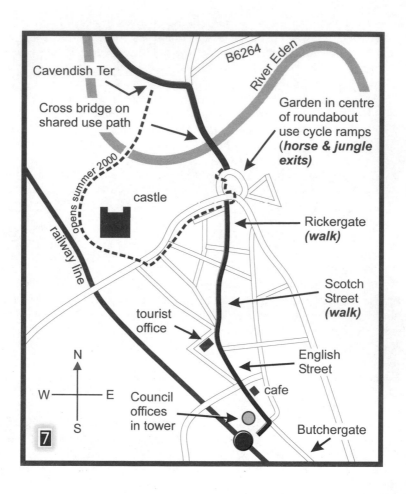

Cavendish Ter

Cross bridge on
shared use path

opens summer 2000

railway line

castle

B6264

River Eden

Garden in centre
of roundabout
use cycle ramps
(*horse & jungle
exits*)

Rickergate
(walk)

Scotch
Street
(walk)

tourist
office

English
Street

cafe

N
W — E
S

Council
offices
in tower

Butchergate

7

ROUTE IN CARLISLE

Carlisle is fairly compact so you'd probably be as well to walk between the railway station and the River Eden; you'd have to walk about half of it anyway as it's pedestrianised. The new cyclepath by the castle should be open by now but crossing the river on the main bridge carrying the A7 is fine too as there are wide shared-use pavements.

The café marked on the map is particularly useful as it has deep glass windows with railings opposite so you can watch your bike and luggage while you are eating. The roundabout shown on the map has a sunken garden area in the middle with ramps leading up and down to the footpaths on either side.

3

EDINBURGH–GLASGOW
(CLYDE TO FORTH CYCLE ROUTE)

TOTAL DISTANCE – 56 MILES
FOR EDINBURGH TO GLASGOW START AT PAGE 64
FOR GLASGOW TO EDINBURGH START AT PAGE 79 AND WORK BACKWARDS

INTRODUCTION

It gives you a lot to think about cycling over this route; whether you start from Edinburgh or Glasgow you get away surprisingly quickly from the city centre. From Glasgow the route follows the banks of the River Clyde, from Edinburgh it's the Water of Leith. In both cases it's along a leafy path but at the Glasgow end you get occasional looks at the urban jungle too: the SECC Exhibition Centre and a steel works.

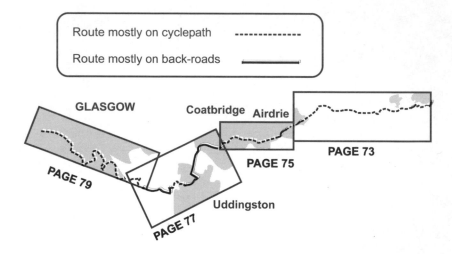

Later on there are a few parts on roads but most of the time you'll be completely away from traffic; dogwalkers might be an occasional hazard and possibly a few fishermen at Hillend Reservoir, but the remote Airdrie to Bathgate section is likely to be very quiet.

An interesting feature of this remote section is a sculpture trail. It starts at Drumgelloch railway station and is 15 miles long; there are specially commissioned sculptures every mile or so on the dedicated cyclepath, not to mention panoramic views of the distant Pentland Hills.

A very attractive area further east is in Almondell Country Park. Here part of the route is on a dirt trail that winds through the woods close to the River Almond.

Inevitably a large proportion of the route is close to urban areas – this is the most highly populated area of Scotland after all. Quite often the National Cycle Network uses cycle trails in public parks in towns, so you won't be cycling through too many shopping malls. Quite a lot of the route through Airdrie is in public parks, and going through Livingston it seems as if it is mostly a public park – providing you don't leave the cycle route that is!

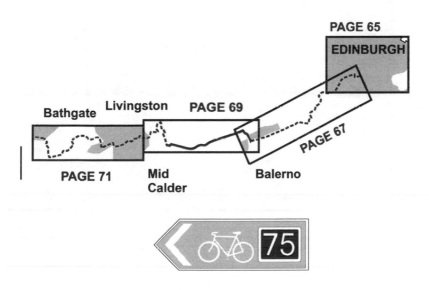

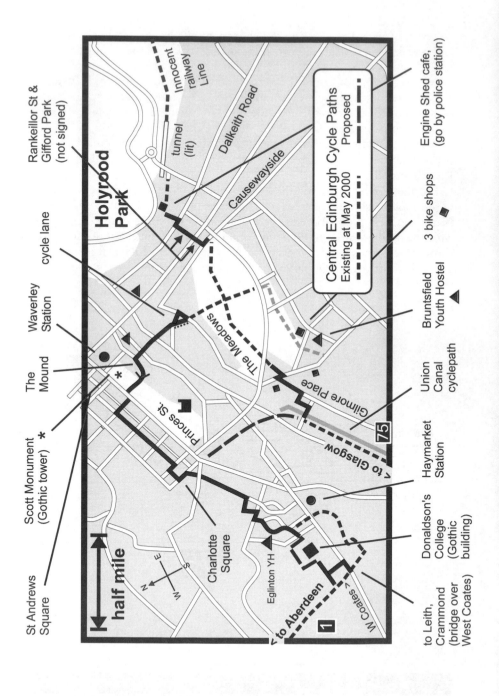

St Andrews Square

Scott Monument (Gothic tower) *

The Mound

Waverley Station

cycle lane

Rankeillor St & Gifford Park (not signed)

Holyrood Park

tunnel (lit)

Innocent railway Line

Dalkeith Road

Causewayside

Central Edinburgh Cycle Paths
Existing at May 2000
Proposed

Engine Shed cafe, (go by police station)

3 bike shops

Bruntsfield Youth Hostel ▲

Union Canal cyclepath

Gilmore Place

to Glasgow

75

Princes St.

Charlotte Square

N E S W

half mile

Eglinton YH ▲

to Aberdeen

W Coates

1

Haymarket Station

Donaldson's College (Gothic building)

to Leith, Crammond (bridge over West Coates)

AROUND EDINBURGH

Edinburgh always was a compact city; until the eighteenth century it was huddled behind the walls of what is now the Old Town. Edinburgh hesitated, but when expansion came in 1767 the New Town was constrained on one side by the Nor' Loch (now Princes Street Gardens). The winner of the architectural competition, James Craig, laid out his elegant squares and streets on the ridge opposite the castle.

When the railway came there was room for it in the now drained Nor' Loch, with tunnels connecting it to Haymarket and Leith. When the motorways arrived it wasn't clear how they could be fitted in so Edinburgh hesitated again, just long enough for it to become clear that perhaps driving elevated dual carriageways over Princes Street and Melville Drive wasn't a good idea after all.

Of course this hasn't stopped the relentless increase in the number of cars. The City Fathers have come round to the realisation that if they can't destroy the Georgian New Town to build roads and don't want to have total gridlock in the city centre, they are just going to have to restrict the number of cars. Unsurprisingly the bicycle has a role here.

What Spokes, the Lothian Cycle Campaign, had been saying for years began to look sensible and Sustrans was employed to draw up a plan. This was Sustrans' first venture in Scotland and it played a key role in their transition from a small pressure group in Bristol to a UK-wide organisation.

The compactness of the city centre has also made it difficult to fit in cyclepaths. From the north and west you can get to within a mile of Princes Street on a former railway line and the Union Canal towpath. After that providing space for cyclists means taking it away from cars. Getting south from the city centre has required a bit more ingenuity.

The National Route terminates at the Royal Bank of Scotland in St Andrew Square (sponsor of the cast iron signs you'll see occasionally). I suggest that if you are arriving in Edinburgh by bicycle from the south or west and looking for accommodation you stay in the area around The Meadows / Tollcross where there is a youth hostel and a good choice of B&Bs; it's only a mile from Princes Street and will be a lot cheaper. Arriving from the north, Eglinton Youth Hostel would be convenient. Book in advance.

Edinburgh is 'full of theatre tricks' said Robert Louis Stevenson: 'You turn a corner, and there is the sun going down on the Highland hills. You look down an alley, and see ships tacking for the Baltic.' It's still like that. Enjoy your time in Edinburgh, try not to bring a car.

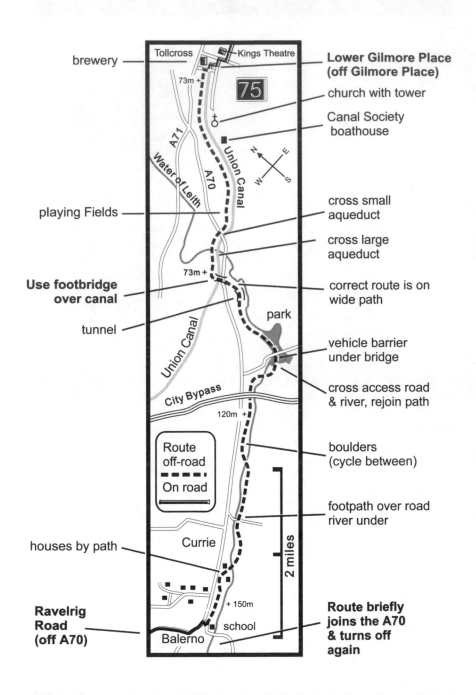

brewery

Tollcross

Kings Theatre

Lower Gilmore Place
(off Gilmore Place)

73m +

75

church with tower

Canal Society
boathouse

A71

Water of Leith

A70

Union Canal

N
E
W
S

playing Fields

cross small
aqueduct

cross large
aqueduct

73m +

Use footbridge
over canal

correct route is on
wide path

park

tunnel

Union Canal

vehicle barrier
under bridge

cross access road
& river, rejoin path

City Bypass

120m +

Route
off-road

On road

boulders
(cycle between)

footpath over road
river under

houses by path

Currie

2 miles

Ravelrig
Road
(off A70)

+ 150m

school

Balerno

Route briefly
joins the A70
& turns off
again

EDINBURGH (TOLLCROSS) TO BALERNO

Tollcross is in central Edinburgh. If you need information about cycle routes from other parts of Edinburgh to Tollcross, refer to maps at the end of Chapter 7 and the start of Chapter 8. This route is labelled the Clyde to Forth Cycle Route by Sustrans; if you want to do it as coast to coast rather than city to city, start in Leith.

This section uses the Union Canal and an old railway by the Water of Leith for a traffic-free route in and out of the city. The Union Canal opened in 1822 and linked Lothian Road, Edinburgh, with lock 16 on the Forth–Clyde Canal. In combination these two canals made it possible to sail from the centre of Edinburgh to the centre of Glasgow. It took all day of course, about the same as it takes to cycle. The Millennium Link project has renewed both canals and their towpaths joining Edinburgh and Glasgow. You might cycle to Glasgow on this route and return on the canal towpath.

The National Route only uses the canal for about two miles. Just west of the aqueduct that carries the canal over the Water of Leith (walk) the route is carried over Lanark Road (the A70) by a footbridge where it joins the former Balerno railway line.

It's about 40 years since trains ran along here; the main piece of evidence that the railway ever existed is the tunnel at the east end – apart from this it now just seems a leafy path by the Water of Leith.

Between 1874 and 1963, though, it echoed with the sound of little steam trains taking people to work from Currie and Balerno and serving the nearby paper mill. On Sundays it was an escape route for city dwellers going to the Pentland Hills or for a picnic by the river. Following it on a bike is easy. If in doubt always follow the wider path.

The path goes all the way to Balerno where it ends by a school. The Sustrans route leaves the dirt path here, turning on to the A70 briefly before joining Ravelrig Road. It's only a short distance on the A70 so walking along the pavement if you have children isn't too much hardship.

In the longer term the cycle route will go round the north of Balerno via Glenbrook. This is not possible at present as the link between the A70 and Easter Newton Farm is missing (see map next page). Naturally when this link is in place it will be signposted to go that way.

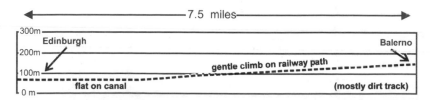

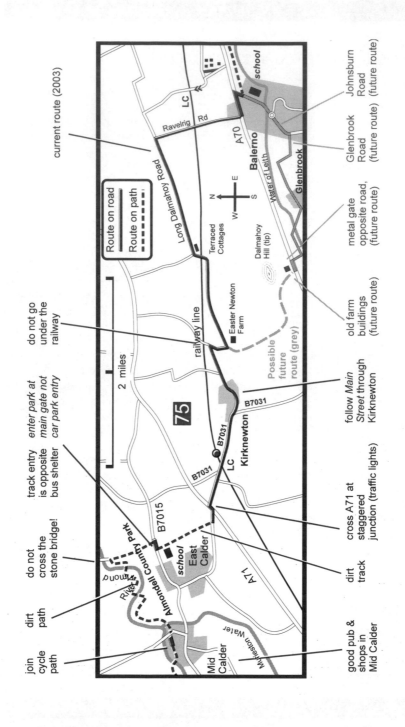

current route (2003)

Route on road
Route on path

do not go
under the
railway

enter park at
main gate not
car park entry

track entry
is opposite
bus shelter

2 miles

75

do not
cross the
stone bridge!

dirt
path

join
cycle
path

follow *Main
Street* through
Kirknewton

cross A71 at
staggered
junction (traffic lights)

dirt
track

good pub &
shops in
Mid Calder

metal gate
opposite road,
(future route)

old farm
buildings
(future route)

Glenbrook
Road
(future route)

Johnsburn
Road
(future route)

Long Dalmahoy Road

Ravelrig Rd

LC

school

A70

Balerno

Water of Leith

Glenbrook

N
W   E
S

Terraced
Cottages

Dalmahoy
Hill (tip)

Easter Newton
Farm

railway line

Possible
future
route (grey)

B7031

Kirknewton

LC

B7031

B7031

B7015

Almondell Country Park

school

East
Calder

River Almond

Mid
Calder

Murieston Water

A71

BALERNO TO ALMONDELL

Most of this section is on farmland, much of it with open views towards the Firth of Forth, the Forth bridges occasionally being visible.

At the Balerno end there's a brief bit on the A70, then a fast descent crossing the Edinburgh–Carstairs railway line on Ravelrig Road. It's not quite so fast going in the other direction – most people would prefer to walk up the hill.

In the longer term the cycle route may go round the north of Balerno via Glenbrook. This is not possible at present as the link between the A70 and Easter Newton Farm is missing. In the meantime it's a back road along Long Dalmahoy Road to Kirknewton.

Kirknewton was a RAF fighter base during the Second World War. The village has several food shops, a pub, but no tea room. There is a public park with swings for children so you could picnic there. Just after Kirknewton you cross the railway again near the train station. You could use this to return to Edinburgh by train.

Use the signals to cross the busy A71. Just east of this it's a dirt track leading to East Calder and Almondell Country Park. Enter the park by the pedestrian entrance, not via the car park.

Almondell is really lovely and is a good destination for a day ride. There is a barbeque site and other attractions. The Union Canal is only a mile or so north-east of Almondell via back roads, so you could return to Edinburgh by the Union Canal towpath if you wanted to do a circular day ride.

The bike route through Almondell remains south of the River Almond. There's an attractive stone bridge, but don't cross over it, continue upstream on the south bank of the river. Towards the Livingston end this is a dirt path winding through trees; interesting, though a mountain bike is not necessary as it has been upgraded.

If you're looking for something to eat the Torphichen Arms in Mid Calder serves food all day and is recommended. There's a small shop opposite too. If you're going through Livingston and looking for food, this will involve a diversion from the route, probably to a shopping mall or fast food outlet.

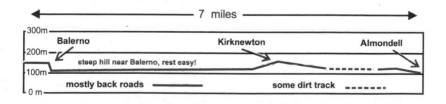

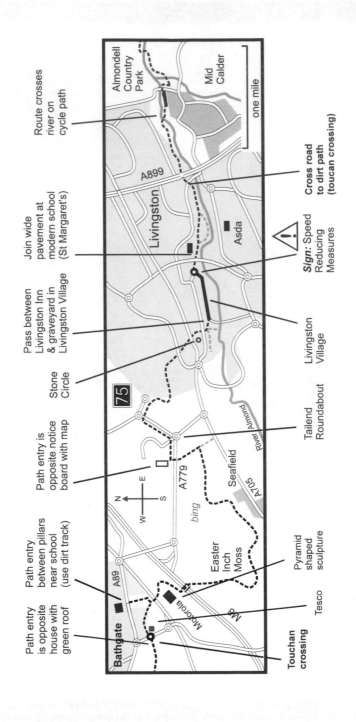

Path entry is opposite house with green roof

Path entry between pillars near school (use dirt track)

Path entry is opposite notice board with map

Pass between Livingston Inn & graveyard in Livingston Village

Stone Circle

Join wide pavement at modern school (St Margaret's)

Route crosses river on cycle path

Bathgate

A89

Tesco

Touchan crossing

Motorola

Pyramid shaped sculpture

Easter Inch Moss

bing

A779

Seafield

A705

M8

River Almond

Tailend Roundabout

Livingston Village

Sign: Speed Reducing Measures

Cross road to dirt path (toucan crossing)

Asda

Livingston

A899

Almondell Country Park

Mid Calder

one mile

75

N
W — E
S

ALMONDELL TO BATHGATE

About half of this section is in the town of Livingston. My most regular visit to Livingston is my annual trip to the Heavy Goods Vehicle Testing Station to get the BikeBus certified for another year of transporting cyclists around Scotland. I have to admit that riding through on the cyclepaths surprised me – most of the time you're in a park and the industrial estates are invisible.

Between Almondell Country Park and Livingston Village the cycle route follows the River Almond on the Almond Path North. Livingston is full of cyclepaths so it's necessary to remember that you are following Route 75 and not go off on to other trails. It's well signposted though so keep looking out for that number. If you do go wrong keep near the river between those two points and you'll get there.

Livingston Village is the only part on a road. Going west look out for the sign: Speed Reducing Measures, and leave at the other end between the Livingston Inn (serves food) and a graveyard. Going east bike along Main Street then bear right at a roundabout to go under the A899 at Quarrywood Court. Stopping for food elsewhere in Livingston will involve a long detour to a shopping mall.

West of Livingston Village the route to follow is Eliburn Campus Path but this is likewise well provided with Route 75 signs. Between Tailend roundabout and the Motorola factory at Bathgate the route crosses Easter Inch Moss. This peat bog was formed after the last Ice Age and is a wildlife reserve; important for breeding and migrant birds, it's also quite scenic. Between it and the A779 there's one of the red-coloured hills known locally as 'bings'.

Bings are actually spoil heaps from shale mining. This was started around 1850 by the inventor of paraffin, James Young Simpson. Shale oil from here was the main world source of petroleum products for a number of years; it was eventually put out of business by the development of the Middle Eastern oil fields.

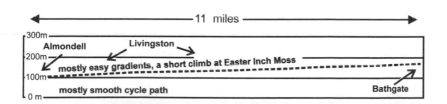

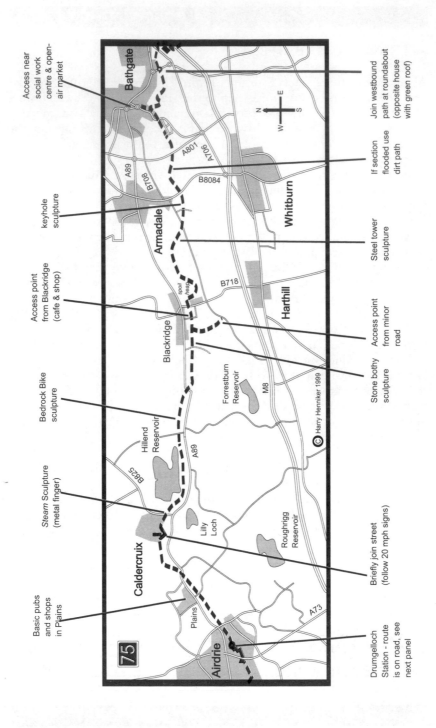

75

Bathgate

Access near social work centre & open-air market

Join westbound path at roundabout (opposite house with green roof)

N
E
W
S

If section flooded use dirt path

A801

A709

B8084

keyhole sculpture

A89

B708

Armadale

Whitburn

Steel tower sculpture

Access point from Blackridge (cafe & shop)

spoil heap

B718

Harthill

Access point from minor road

Blackridge

Stone bothy sculpture

Bedrock Bike sculpture

Forrestburn Reservoir

M8

© Harry Henniker 1999

Hillend Reservoir

A89

B825

Steam Sculpture (metal finger)

Lilly Loch

Caldercruix

Roughrigg Reservoir

Briefly join street (follow 20 mph signs)

Basic pubs and shops in Plains

Plains

A73

Airdrie

Drumgelloch Station - route is on road, see next panel

BATHGATE TO AIRDRIE

I haven't mapped this part in great detail as finding your way is simply a matter of following the railway path. This 15-mile traffic-free route across Scotland's central plateau was originally built in the 1850s as the Airdrie–Bathgate Junction Railway. Its main purpose was to carry coal and limestone to numerous works in the Monkland district.

This district is notable for having the first steam-powered railway in Scotland, the Monkland and Kirkintilloch which opened only a year after the Stockton to Darlington in England.

Mining for coal is of course still a living memory in the central belt. While researching this book I was cycling along near Caldercruix and met a retired miner on his bike. He was 74, he said, and for much of his youth he had biked between Caldercruix and Whitburn to work at Polkemmet Colliery. He thought the cyclepath was a great thing and had recently got a bike again and cycled for two hours most days – over much the same route.

In addition to the views this section is interesting for the sculpture trail which it incorporates. The sculptures all have some connection with the history of the area you're passing through. The aim has been to have art in public places so that everyone can enjoy it. It's just as well they are strongly constructed.

There has been a lot of tree planting by the Central Scotland Forest Trust who are developing the Central Scotland Forest in the area.

It's probably a good idea to bear in mind that this part of the cycle route is rather exposed and quite remote. The weather can change suddenly even in summer, so have at least a sweater and a waterproof jacket with you. Between Bathgate and Airdrie the only places that could offer food and shelter are Armadale and Plains (pubs and shops only, no café). Hillend Reservoir is a good spot for a picnic.

This section ends at Drumgelloch Station, at which point it is possible to catch a train to Glasgow.

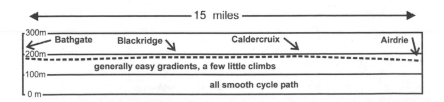

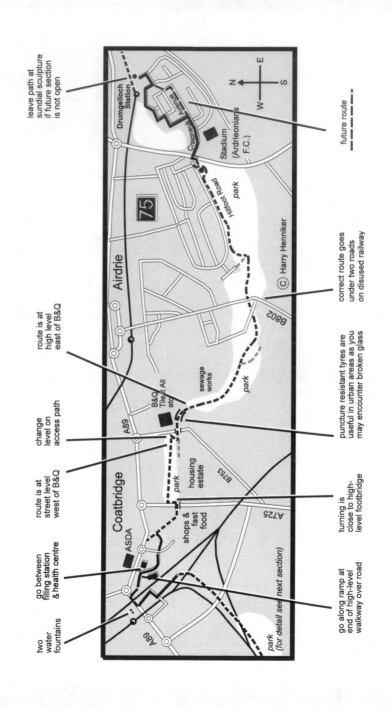

leave path at sundial sculpture if future section is not open

Drumgelloch Station

Craigneuk Avenue

Stadium (Ardrieonians F.C.)

future route

75

Airdrie

© Harry Henniker

correct route goes under two roads on disused railway

Hilltoot Road

park

B802

park

route is at high level east of B&Q

change level on access path

B&Q Tile it All etc

sewage works

puncture resistant tyres are useful in urban areas as you may encounter broken glass

route is at street level west of B&Q

A89

park

housing estate

B753

turning is close to high-level footbridge

A725

Coatbridge

go between filling station & health centre

ASDA

shops & fast food

two water fountains

A89

go along ramp at end of high-level walkway over road

park (for detail see next section)

N
W — E
S

AIRDRIE TO COATBRIDGE

Drumgelloch Station on the west side of Airdrie is the point where currently the sculpture trail of the bike path turns into ordinary streets. This junction is marked by a sculpture which doubles as a sundial.

At the time of writing it was necessary to join or leave the bike path by the sundial, as the bike path extension beyond the station was just a fenced-off mound of earth. It's worth going the extra 50 metres beyond the sundial just to check though – they might have finished it by the time you get there. Don't leave the station by the train platform, this will take you on to a maze of streets on the north side of the railway – entirely the wrong way.

West of Airdrieonians Football Stadium, by a Burger King, the route turns into paths in a park; the route between here and central Coatbridge is entirely on these paths. If you find yourself going along a street you've gone wrong. Remember to change levels near the B&Q superstore (see map).

Some of Coatbridge's industrial heritage is preserved in Summerlee Industrial Museum, but most of the rest of it is now submerged in shopping malls and fast food outlets. The cyclepath makes use of where the Monklands Canal used to be and the former railway lines along which every steel mill and factory had to import raw materials and export finished goods.

Not all of the bike path is prettied up – some of it runs through disused ground which the council has not worked on yet. At the time of writing Sustrans had not found a path ranger for the Coatbridge area so parts of the bike route were quite untidy.

The area between the Asda filling station and Coatbridge railway station is quite complex and the cycle route signs tend to be swamped by all the shop signs and other street hardware. Take it slowly and look out for the two fountains near the train station where you have to make the turn (see map). If you do stray off the route and have to ask for directions you may find that the person you speak to is unaware that there is a cycle route in the area. In this situation it is probably best to ask for a local landmark on the route: B&Q, football stadium etc.

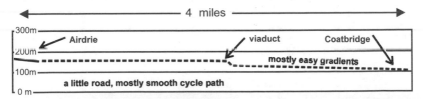

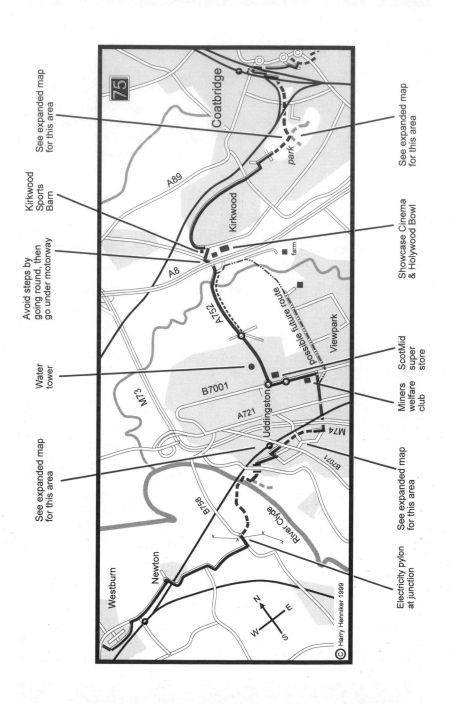

75

Coatbridge

See expanded map for this area

See expanded map for this area

Kirkwood Sports Barn

A89

Kirkwood

park

Showcase Cinema & Holywood Bowl

Avoid steps by going round, then go under motorway

A8

farm

A752

possible future route

Water tower

B7001

Viewpark

ScotMid super store

M73

Uddingston

A721

Miners welfare club

M74

B7071

See expanded map for this area

See expanded map for this area

Electricity pylon at junction

B758

River Clyde

Westburn

Newton

N
W — E
S

© Harry Henniker 1999

COATBRIDGE TO WESTBURN

Between Coatbridge and Uddingston the bike route has to pass under the M8 (A8) motorway. It does this near the Showcase Cinema and the Holywood Bowl complex just east of junction 8. Currently the route either side of this uses roads, though Sustrans is currently working on path alternatives. These are indicated on the map and will be signposted on opening.

Route Detail Coatbridge- -Kirkwood

At present the route has to use the A752 just south of the M8. The local council have made the footpath wider, so use it.

The original meaning of Uddingston was Oda's Farm. It's quite a residential area these days and the route through it is a mixture of bike path and minor roads. It is quite complex, so if the odd signpost is missing you could go astray. Pay attention to the map! I went through in the autumn and the whole place was covered in leaves which had temporarily made some of the bike path invisible. West of Uddingston the route is quite pretty where it crosses the River Clyde on a footbridge.

Route Detail - Uddingston

Between Uddingston and Bell's Bridge the only easy opportunity to get a cup of tea will be at the Safeway near Cambuslang, where there is a very reasonable café inside the supermarket (see map on p. 76). If you feel the need for refreshment in Uddingston visit one of the establishments on Main Street.

The route around Newton and Westburn has no particular attraction, though there are open views towards Glasgow and the Campsie Fells to the north.

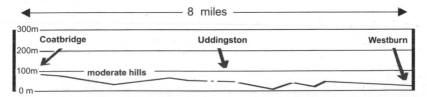

8 miles

300m
200m
100m
0 m

Coatbridge   Uddingston   Westburn

moderate hills

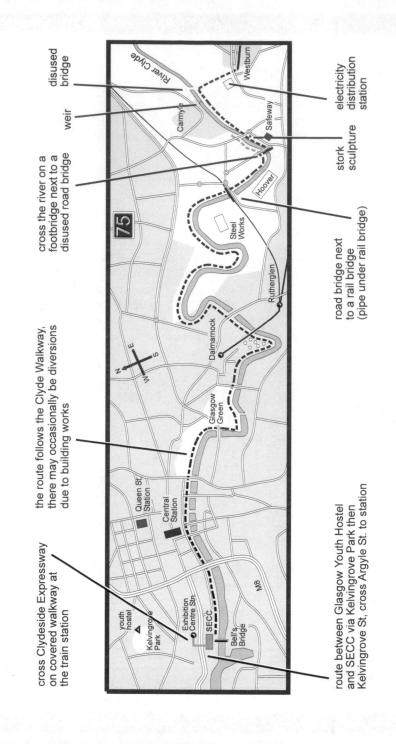

River Clyde

disused bridge

electricity distribution station

weir

Carmyle

Westburn

Safeway

stork sculpture

75

cross the river on a footbridge next to a disused road bridge

Hoover

Steel Works

road bridge next to a rail bridge (pipe under rail bridge)

Rutherglen

the route follows the Clyde Walkway, there may occasionally be diversions due to building works

Dalmarnock

N
E
S
W

Glasgow Green

Queen St Station

Central Station

cross Clydeside Expressway on covered walkway at the train station

M8

youth hostel

Kelvingrove Park

Exhibition Centre Stn

SECC

Bell's Bridge

route between Glasgow Youth Hostel and SECC via Kelvingrove Park then Kelvingrove St, cross Argyle St. to station

WESTBURN TO GLASGOW

This section is entirely on bike paths, though there may be the odd diversion on the Clyde Walkway due to building works. The bike path ends or starts at Bell's Bridge, the pedestrian and cyclist's bridge that is a hub of the Scottish Cycle Network; on the other side of the river bike routes run south to Kilwinning, Ardrossan, Ayr and eventually Carlisle.

The cyclepath by the banks of the Clyde is at times quite leafy and pretty but you never lose sight of the fact that you are in the middle of a big city. The route passes through Glasgow Green – the large ornate building on the city side is Templeton's Carpet Factory. When James Templeton sought permission to build a carpet factory by the park the City Fathers refused permission for a common factory. The result was a building modelled on the Doge's Palace in Venice. Bonnie Prince Charlie reviewed his troops on the Green, though it's understood that he wasn't particularly welcome locally.

Another landmark near Bell's Bridge is the Finnieston Crane, built in 1932 to load steam locomotives on to ships for export to India, China, South Africa and the United States. Some years ago one of these locomotives returned and can be seen near the bike route at the Summerlee Heritage Centre in Coatbridge.

Probably you'll end or start your journey at Bell's Bridge, and if that's the case you might be looking for accommodation. Glasgow SYHA youth hostel is quite near, and the best way to get there is to walk to Kelvingrove Park, then up through the park; on the way you'll also pass a number of independent hostels (see Appendix).

If you've come from Edinburgh you could consider an alternative route to cycle back. This uses towpaths on the Forth–Clyde canal and the Union Canal. Just follow the canals. A more detailed description of the canal route is given in my other book, *101 Bike Routes in Scotland*.

The Union Canal is no longer broken by the M8, so you can follow it right in to Edinburgh. One way to get to the Forth–Clyde Canal from Bell's Bridge is to follow the Glasgow–Loch Lomond–Inverness route until it reaches the canal towpath (then turn right).

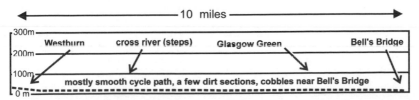

AROUND GLASGOW

GLASGOW: Scotland's largest city and one-time second city of the British Empire, even if not Scotland's capital. The map opposite gives an overview of the Sustrans cycle routes in the immediate vicinity of Glasgow.

Mostly they make use of former railway lines, with the occasional quiet street to link them up. Sometimes there are purpose-built linking sections where Sustrans has been able to obtain the right to build a dedicated cyclepath.

The Edinburgh–Glasgow route is numbered 75 by Sustrans. They call it the Clyde–Forth Cycle Route and extend it to Greenock via Paisley; at the Edinburgh end it finishes in Leith. This section, between Glasgow and Greenock, is in the Glasgow–Carlisle chapter of this book to avoid me having to put the Glasgow–Paisley cycle route maps in twice.

The fact that Glasgow is larger than Edinburgh is due to its position on Scotland's Atlantic seaboard. The initial phase of Glasgow's dramatic expansion was between 1750 and 1776 and was based on the tobacco trade with the British North American colonies. This declined with the American Declaration of Independence.

At this point the tobacco lords of Glasgow were awash with money and they needed to do something with it. The answer was the cotton trade. The West Indies provided the raw material and local linen weavers quickly moved to cotton. The industry went from hand power, to water power, to steam power. By 1812 the cotton industry employed 151,300 people with 120 spinning mills.

The final phase of Glasgow's spectacular growth was based on ship building and heavy engineering. Between 1851 and 1870 the Clyde produced an amazing 70 per cent of all iron ships built in Britain. The Clyde maintained its technical lead until 1914, and expanded into railway locomotive building, machine tools and many other types of heavy industry.

Providing proper housing for the people of Glasgow was never a priority with the tobacco lords (with one notable exception: Robert Owen), or even the cotton or ship building barons. Nor, mostly, did they pay high enough wages to enable their workers to buy a house or even pay a decent rent.

Latterly Glasgow Council coped with this the best it could by creating working-class dormitory suburbs: Drumchapel, Easterhouse, Castlemilk, Pollok and Priesthill (not even a pub before 1969). You'll cycle past some of these aesthetic disasters on your way in or out of Glasgow. Some of the tower blocks have been pulled down, others modernised.

Glasgow has some of the best art galleries and museums in Britain and is the home town of architect Charles Rennie Macintosh. There's a series of cultural festivals: Celtic, jazz, folk – the place just bounces with energy. Politically it's been a fervently socialist city, but what exactly this means today is getting a bit lost. It's said that the people of Edinburgh and Glasgow are very different – you'll be in a position to judge this for yourself. As I'm from Edinburgh I'm saying nothing!

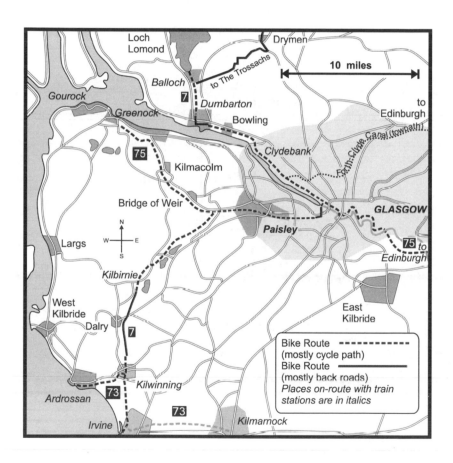

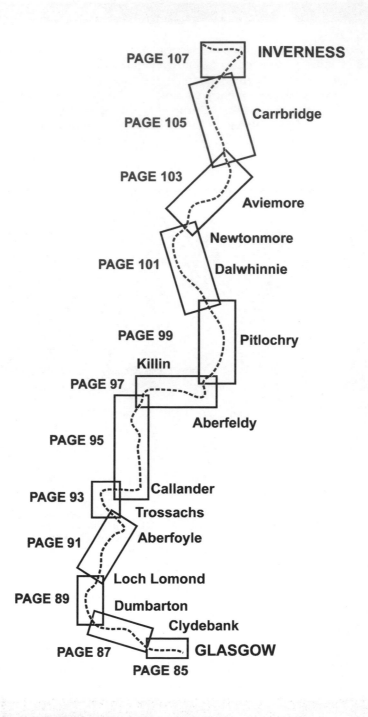

4

GLASGOW–INVERNESS
(LOCH AND GLENS NORTH)

TOTAL DISTANCE – 214 MILES (21 MILES TO LOCH LOMOND)
FOR GLASGOW TO INVERNESS SEE PAGE 84
FOR INVERNESS TO GLASGOW SEE PAGE 107 AND WORK BACKWARDS

INTRODUCTION

This is the main route through the central Highlands. It passes through Caledonian pine forests, by some of the most scenic glens in Scotland and takes in the lochs Tay, Earn, Lubnaig and Vennachar.

While cycling in the Highlands has always been popular, a problem in recent years has been the increase in motor traffic. This is particularly so in the Highlands due to the limited number of roads. For this route, this is something that is no longer a problem because these busy sections are now avoided by dedicated cyclepaths.

The National Cycle Network routes through Glen Ogle and the Drumochter Pass are two of the most ambitious that Sustrans has ever undertaken. Along these sections you can cycle through the mountain scenery without meeting any cars.

This has completely transformed the situation and the route should become as popular as the C2C route between Workington and Tynemouth in the north of England. It certainly should be well used because the scenery it passes through is as lovely as any in Europe and there is no lack of interesting things to see: castles, waterfalls and mountains by the score.

Most of the towns and villages on the route are well served by B&Bs, hotels, youth hostels and bunk houses so there are plenty of places to stay. There's also lots of historic interest – the end-game of Bonnie Prince Charlie's reckless adventure in Scotland, Flodden Battlefield, is on the route, together with Ruthven Barracks – built to ensure that sort of thing couldn't happen.

You should be prepared for some long hills, though generally the gradients are quite reasonable. Warm waterproof clothing is essential at any time of year on the higher sections. Between Pitlochry and Inverness the route is quite well served by railway stations though trains are less frequent than in more populated areas. If you are using the train to start or finish, reserve a space for your bike as these are limited.

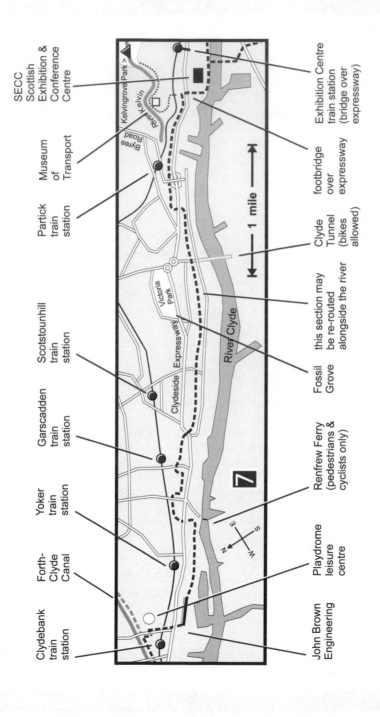

Clydebank
train
station

Forth-
Clyde
Canal

Yoker
train
station

Garscadden
train
station

Scotstounhill
train
station

Partick
train
station

Museum
of
Transport

SECC
Scottish
Exhibition &
Conference
Centre

John Brown
Engineering

Playdrome
leisure
centre

Renfrew Ferry
(pedestrians &
cyclists only)

Fossil
Grove

this section may
be re-routed
alongside the river

Clyde
Tunnel
(bikes
allowed)

footbridge
over
expressway

Exhibition Centre
train station
(bridge over
expressway)

— 1 mile —

Kelvingrove Park >

River Kelvin

Byres Road

Clydeside Expressway

Victoria Park

River Clyde

7

N
W   E
S

BELL'S BRIDGE TO CLYDEBANK

The Glasgow end starts from Bell's Bridge near the Scottish Exhibition and Conference Centre (SECC). Routes from here go south to Ayr and Carlisle, west to Gourock and east to Edinburgh.

The Glasgow to Loch Lomond section was opened in 1989 and was the first long-distance cycleway in Scotland. Between Clydebank and Bell's Bridge the route is near the Clyde, west of this it joins the Forth–Clyde Canal towpath. At the Bell's Bridge end the route begins by crossing over the Clydeside Expressway; this is very near but after a while there is a narrow park and the roar of traffic subsides.

Train stations are all along the route. This is convenient, as you can hop on a train with your bike to get home at the end of the day. They are mostly well signposted from the route; if you see signs saying, say Partick or Yoker, with a bike symbol, this will be the route to the station and not the main cycle route.

There are some interesting things to see along here; the Finnieston Crane, used to lift giant steam locomotives and the Museum of Transport in Kelvin Hall, which has some fine old Glasgow tram cars as well as early bicycles – there's a café too.

West of the River Kelvin it's obvious that the route is following an old railway line, but some of the bridges have been lost and the path dips. Quite near here is Victoria Park, built on the site of an old quarry. There are some lovely rock gardens and an arboretum. Particularly famous is Fossil Grove, with petrified tree stumps 250 million years old. The Renfrew pedestrian and cycle ferry is quite near; on the Renfrew side a cycle link by White Cart Water joins up to Sustrans Route 7 to Paisley and beyond. This could make a circular route within Glasgow.

At the west end of this section the cyclepath leaves the former Lanarkshire–Dunbartonshire railway line and transfers to the Forth–Clyde Canal towpath. This is near Clydebank train station; a useful landmark here is the modern Playdrome building which has swimming pools, flumes, sport facilities and a restaurant. You join the canal near a mock ocean liner – Monagles Fish Restaurant.

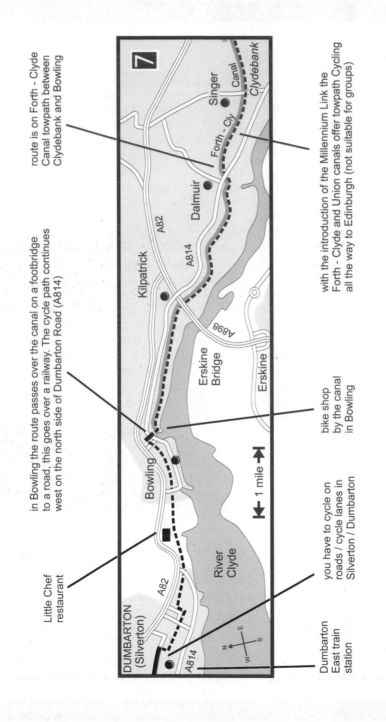

7

route is on Forth - Clyde Canal towpath between Clydebank and Bowling

in Bowling the route passes over the canal on a footbridge to a road, this goes over a railway. The cycle path continues west on the north side of Dumbarton Road (A814)

Little Chef restaurant

DUMBARTON (Silverton)

River Clyde

Bowling

Kilpatrick

A82

A814

Dalmuir

Singer

Forth - Cly

Canal

Clydebank

Forth - Cly Canal

A82

A814

A898

Erskine Bridge

Erskine

1 mile

N
W — E
S

bike shop by the canal in Bowling

Dumbarton East train station

you have to cycle on roads / cycle lanes in Silverton / Dumbarton

with the introduction of the Millennium Link the Forth - Clyde and Union canals offer towpath Cycling all the way to Edinburgh (not suitable for groups)

CLYDEBANK TO DUMBARTON

The canal towpath is quite wide, with a good dirt surface, and west of Clydebank it's attractive with swans and ducks and views of people's back gardens as you roll along. At the Clydebank end there is a large shopping mall which includes a coffee shop. Finding somewhere safe to lock your bike here could be a problem – there's a Little Chef restaurant by the route a mile west of Bowling which might be better.

Clydebank Museum, run by Dunbartonshire Council, is interesting. It has displays about the Roman army building the Antonine Wall and 2000 years later, the building of the great ships *Queen Mary* and *Queen Elizabeth*. Opening hours are limited however.

On the way to Bowling you pass under the Erskine Bridge; its deck is 180 feet above the river but it was still seriously damaged some years ago when a ship passed under it. They had made a miscalculation about the height of the tide – the resulting closure and restrictions caused all sorts of traffic problems in Glasgow.

At the west end the canal section terminates at the old Customs house in Bowling. This indicates the past importance of the canal. To see the canal basin and the sea, go through the railway arches. There's a bike shop under the arches. The massive railway swing bridge isn't used by the cyclepath, so you have to cross a road (see map).

Between Bowling and Dumbarton there's another Little Chef restaurant (see map on p. 86). Nearer to Dumbarton is Dumbarton Castle. Dumbarton was capital of the ancient Kingdom of Strathclyde and the castle was important as a stronghold controlling entry to the west of Scotland. Also in Dumbarton is the Denny Tank, part of the Scottish Maritime Museum. The clipper ship *Cutty Sark* (see also Ayr page) was built in Denny. The tank was built in 1881 for testing ship hull designs.

Between Dumbarton East train station and the River Leven the route takes to back roads to get through the town. There is a short busy section in central Dumbarton, see map on next page.

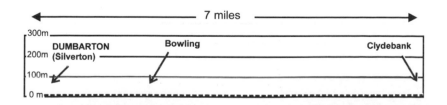

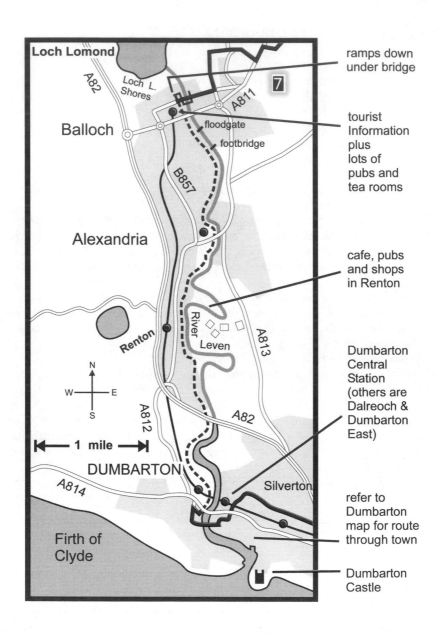

Loch Lomond

Loch L. Shores

A82

A811

7

ramps down under bridge

Balloch

floodgate

footbridge

tourist Information plus lots of pubs and tea rooms

B857

Alexandria

cafe, pubs and shops in Renton

River Leven

A813

Renton

Dumbarton Central Station (others are Dalreoch & Dumbarton East)

N
W   E
S

A812

A82

1 mile

DUMBARTON

Silverton

refer to Dumbarton map for route through town

A814

Firth of Clyde

Dumbarton Castle

DUMBARTON TO BALLOCH (LOCH LOMOND)

Dumbarton is a busy little place but the cycle route is well signposted, and if any signs are missing refer to the map. Note that you should not go on to the A814 / Glasgow Road near the bridge but turn down a side road to the park (see map).

North of Dumbarton the route follows the west bank of the River Leven. It passes under the A82 dual carriageway and north of this it meanders prettily over little wooden bridges keeping by the river most of the time. The scenery is attractive but this is not always the case with the built-up environment.

The River Leven is fast flowing and was important at one time for water-powered industry; plinths near the route explain the natural features. The path should be quiet but is shared with pedestrians, occasionally it joins access roads – where this occurs keep by the river.

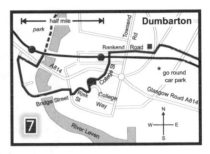

Balloch, at the south end of Loch Lomond, is the termination point of the railway line. It's got lots of shops and cafés; the train station and tourist office are at the end of the cyclepath. There's a picnic site north of the tourist office. Even if you are stopping here and not continuing further north it would be worth continuing along the Sustrans route a little further as this leads to Balloch Castle Country Park. There are views over Loch Lomond and lots of space for the kids to run around – you can always get a train back to Glasgow. The cycle route skirts the Loch Lomond shores development. This is mostly a shopping complex but it includes the Loch Lomond Experience. In my view the best Loch Lomond experience is on a bicycle.

Loch Lomond, famed in song and story, crosses the Highland boundary fault; at its south end are the lower hills of the lowlands, further north is mighty Ben Lomond, a long ridge rising to 3,194 feet. You get more views of this further north. If you're going further north you'll also be crossing the

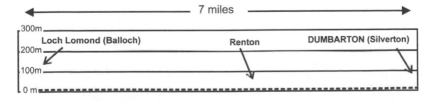

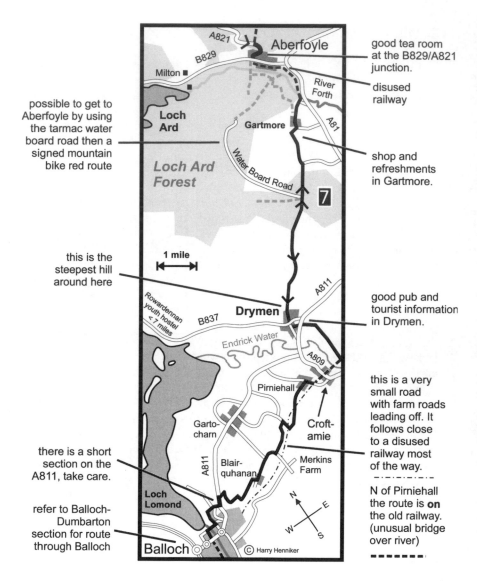

good tea room at the B829/A821 junction.

disused railway

possible to get to Aberfoyle by using the tarmac water board road then a signed mountain bike red route

shop and refreshments in Gartmore.

this is the steepest hill around here

1 mile

good pub and tourist information in Drymen.

this is a very small road with farm roads leading off. It follows close to a disused railway most of the way.

N of Pirniehall the route is **on** the old railway. (unusual bridge over river)

there is a short section on the A811, take care.

refer to Balloch-Dumbarton section for route through Balloch

© Harry Henniker

Highland Boundary Fault near Drymen – you won't need me to point it out. The long-distance walking route, the West Highland Way, passes up the east side of Loch Lomond. A few parts of it can be cycled on a mountain bike, but by Loch Lomond you'd have to carry your bike for nine miles.

BALLOCH TO ABERFOYLE

At the Balloch end you go along a minor road just north of the A811, then turn left towards Balloch Country Park. After that it's quiet minor roads most of the way to Drymen (pronounced Drimmen). There's a very short section on the A811 which needs care. Going north you haven't got to the serious hills yet but there is a general climb. The hills ahead to the right are the Campsie Fells and to the left there are sometimes good views towards Loch Lomond. Between Balloch and Croftamie there is no place to get food or drink.

To the north of here in the hills it's MacGregor Country – Rob Roy and all that. As you can see around here it's still fat-farming country. The lowland farmers here suffered much from cattle thieving in the seventeenth and eighteenth centuries, and it eventually reached the extent that Rob Roy operated a protection racket. The proper authorities were helpless.

An interesting place to stay near Drymen is in the timber 'wigwams'. They offer low cost accommodation on a sleeping platform – indoor camping if you like. Drymen itself is a pleasant village with several good pubs, hotels and B&Bs, and there's also a good choice of shops.

Going north from Drymen just go up the steepest hill you can see and you'll be on the correct route; coming south into Drymen check your brakes before you begin the descent as the hill ends right in the village.

Going north from the top of the hill all routes lead to Aberfoyle. If you've got all day you could explore the mountain bike routes in Loch Ard Forest, other than that the Water Board road is quite straightforward (it's the only tarmac road leading west), and Sustrans offers a new railway path which avoids the A81 and A821.

Aberfoyle is mostly a tourist town, with a tourist office. It's also heavily favoured by walkers and mountain bikers out for the day from one of the towns of the central belt. The tea room by the A821 / B829 junction is recommended. In winter the tea rooms will be closed but the food shop near the car park does refreshments.

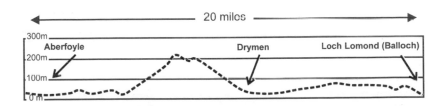

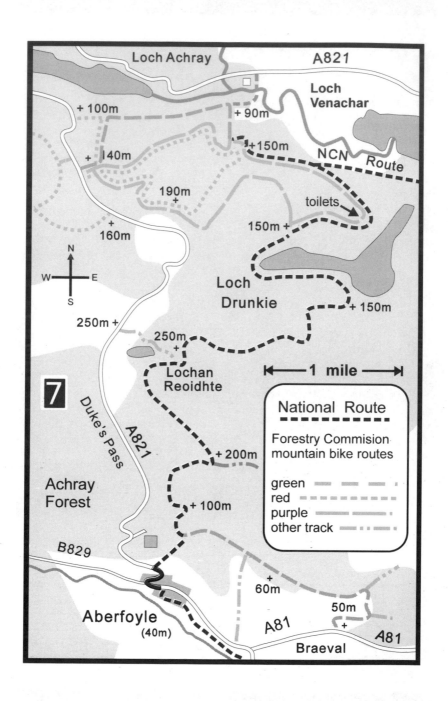

ABERFOYLE TO LOCH VENACHAR

The reason the map opposite looks slightly different is that it's taken from my other book, *101 Mountain Bike Routes in Scotland*. The route Sustrans follows through the forest is also marked as a green-marker mountain bike route by the Forestry Commission. It can be a bit bumpy in places depending on whether they have been extracting timber recently. Part of the route is a forest drive so look out for cars.

Some sections could be closed if they are extracting timber and they don't usually bother taking the signs down on Sundays, even though the Forestry Commission don't usually work then. Some parts could be muddy if there has been recent heavy rain. Generally though it's a good-quality forest dirt road; cycling up on the A821 over the Duke's Pass is OK too as traffic will be slow moving.

Loch Drunkie is a good spot for a picnic; there is a hotel doing bar lunches not too far away at Loch Achray, and an attractive restaurant in between lochs Achray and Vennachar (box symbol on map).

If you have the time for a detour a brilliant little bike ride is the path round Loch Katrine. There are no cars as it's a Water Board road; start from Aberfoyle on the B829 and just keep going. You come out at Loch Achray after 24 miles, and there's only a single turn to make, a right turn at a T-junction going round clockwise.

There is also a little steamer on Loch Katrine, built by the same people who made *Cutty Sark*, the SS *Sir Walter Scott*. It takes bikes, so you could sail up the loch and cycle back.

At the north end of this section the National Route runs east towards Callander on the south side of Loch Venachar. This is really lovely, meandering through trees by the shore. Eventually it gets to a back road which runs into Callander.

Just east of Loch Venachar, just before you get to Callander there is an excellent independent hostel (Wheels), which also does bike hire. Callander itself of course has a big choice of B&Bs and a Rob Roy Centre presenting a rather pasturised image of the ruffian. It and the tourist office are in a converted church.

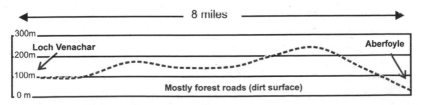

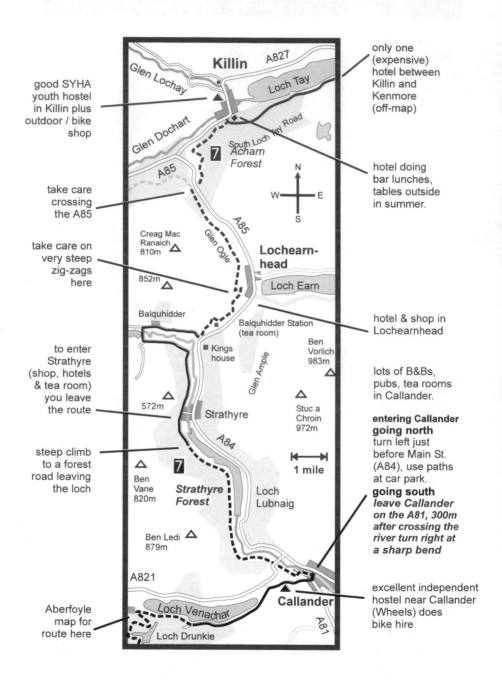

Killin A827

Glen Lochay

Loch Tay

Glen Dochart

A85

Glen Lochay

good SYHA youth hostel in Killin plus outdoor / bike shop

only one (expensive) hotel between Killin and Kenmore (off-map)

7 *Acharn Forest*

South Loch Tay Road

hotel doing bar lunches, tables outside in summer.

N
W   E
S

take care crossing the A85

Creag Mac Ranaich 810m △

Glen Ogle

A85

Lochearn-head

852m △

Loch Earn

take care on very steep zig-zags here

Balquhidder

Balquhidder Station (tea room)

hotel & shop in Lochearnhead

■ Kings house

Glen Ample

Ben Vorlich 983m △

to enter Strathyre (shop, hotels & tea room) you leave the route

572m △

Strathyre

Stuc a Chroin 972m △

lots of B&Bs, pubs, tea rooms in Callander.

A84

entering Callander going north turn left just before Main St. (A84), use paths at car park.

|← 1 mile →|

steep climb to a forest road leaving the loch

7

Ben Vane 820m △

Strathyre Forest

Loch Lubnaig

going south leave Callander on the A81, 300m after crossing the river turn right at a sharp bend

Ben Ledi 879m △

A821

Aberfoyle map for route here

Loch Venachar

Callander

A81

excellent independent hostel near Callander (Wheels) does bike hire

Loch Drunkie

CALLANDER TO KILLIN

This is mostly on cyclepath and it passes through some of the most beautiful scenery in Scotland.

At the north end at Killin the route starts at a forest access point by the Falls of Dochart, where there is a Water Board sign. There are a number of ways through Acharn Forest; the cycle route uses the low one which is partly along a dismantled railway. Higher level routes give good views of Loch Tay and still more or less come out at the same place.

At the south end in Callander there are several signs indicating the route; one of them is quite near the Dreadnought Hotel which is unmistakable. Bear in mind, if you have young children with you, that the route crosses the A821 just north of Callander. You can get food at Strathyre at the Kingshouse Hotel and at Lochearnhead. There is also a restaurant a mile north of the Kingshouse, at Balquhidder station.

Much of this route is on the former railway line of the Caledonian Railway Company. This was never a terribly successful operation – they were plagued by rock falls on to the line when it went up Glen Ogle and had to send an engine up early in the morning to check it out before they ran a scheduled service. The route contour shown below reflects the gradient on the road; the railway is less steep as it climbs gently up the side of the glen.

Rob Roy's grave is on the route at a little church in Balquhidder. His wife is also buried there, and a fragment of poetry on a wall near her grave indicates that perhaps she was a gentler soul than the man himself:

LOVE ALL YOU MEET – NO SEASON KNOWS NOR CLIME,
NOR DAYS, WEEKS, MONTHS – WHICH ARE THE RAGS OF TIME.

Rob Roy's epitaph is shorter:

DESPITE THEM.

There's a tourist office in Killin and a friendly youth hostel, and the Killin Hotel does excellent food. Shutters Restaurant is good too. There is a general outdoor shop in Killin that hires bikes, canoes etc. They should have some of the more common cycle spares.

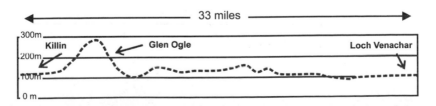

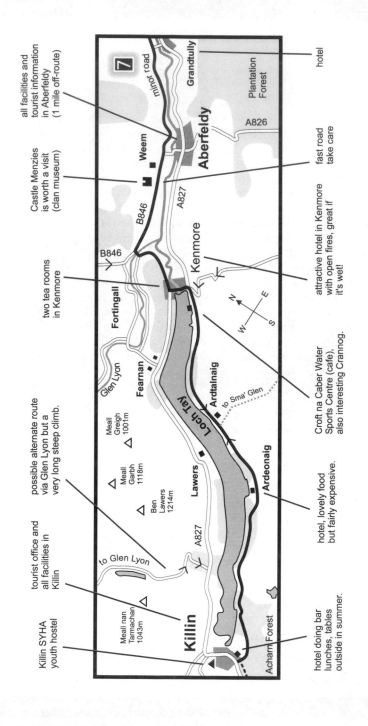

all facilities and tourist information in Aberfeldy (1 mile off-route)

hotel

Castle Menzies is worth a visit (clan museum)

fast road take care

two tea rooms in Kenmore

attractive hotel in Kenmore with open fires, great if it's wet!

Croft na Caber Water Sports Centre (cafe), also interesting Crannog.

possible alternate route via Glen Lyon but a very long steep climb.

tourist office and all facilities in Killin

hotel, lovely food but fairly expensive.

Killin SYHA youth hostel

hotel doing bar lunches, tables outside in summer.

7

minor road

Grandtully

Weem

Aberfeldy

Plantation Forest

A826

A827

B846

Kenmore

B846

Fortingall

Glen Lyon

Fearnan

Loch Tay

Ardtalnaig

to Sma' Glen

N
W E
S

Meall Greigh 1001m

Meall Garbh 1118m

Ben Lawers 1214m

Lawers

Ardeonaig

A827

to Glen Lyon

Meall nan Tarmachan 1043m

Killin

Acharn Forest

KILLIN TO GRANDTULLY

The route leaves Killin on the south Loch Tay road which is beside the Falls of Dochart. Loch Tay, while not quite as large as Loch Lomond, is still a big loch. On the north side is the Ben Lawers range, with some of the grandest mountains in Scotland – Meall nan Tarmachan which towers over Killin, Ben Lawers and Meall Garbh further east. The south Loch Tay road gives excellent views.

The Ardeonaig Hotel, roughly halfway along the loch, does beautiful food but is not cheap. No doubt they could also produce coffee and shortbread if that's more within your budget. The Croft na Caber watersports centre just west of Kenmore has a café with good filled rolls and cakes, and there's a choice of places in Kenmore.

Also next to Croft na Caber is the Scottish Crannog Centre; it has a reproduction *crannog* by Edinburgh University and displays inside. There were crannogs at one time in lochs all over Scotland. Crannogs are settlements on water erected on stilts, and were presumably built because in uncertain times they offered a certain measure of security. Apart from this one they all date from 2000 years ago or more. If you'd like more information I'm sure they'll tell you inside.

If you think you'd like to explore a bit more in this area a good place to start would be Glen Lyon (see map). Glen Lyon is one of the loveliest and longest glens in Scotland and isn't particularly hilly, though the exits at the western end of the glen are spectacularly steep. At the east end is Fortingall, reputedly the birth place of Pontius Pilate who was possibly conceived while his father was sorting out the Picts.

Between Kenmore and Grandtully the route takes to a minor road then crosses the River Lyon to the B846; it passes Castle Menzies, which has now been restored as a Clan Centre. This is a fine example of a Z-plan castle where defence of the walls is covered by projecting towers on diagonally opposite sides. The inside is a bit sparse.

There's a hotel in Weem, and most other amenities slightly off-route across the River Tay in the town of Aberfeldy. Getting to Aberfeldy you'll cross on General Wade's Bridge. There's a restored water mill and a distillery in Aberfeldy. There are two hotels in Grandtully.

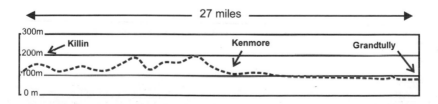

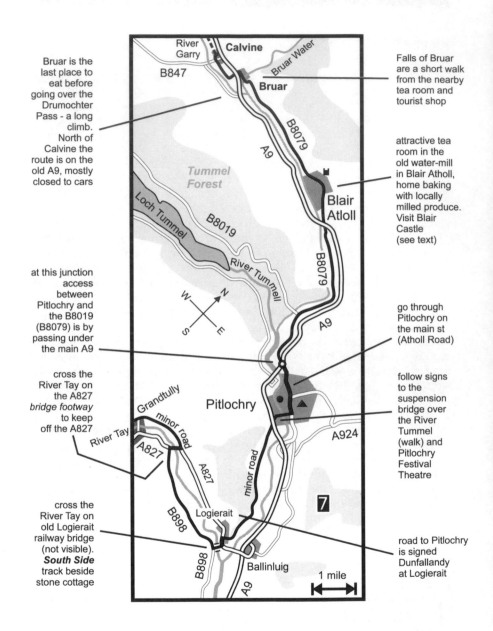

Bruar is the last place to eat before going over the Drumochter Pass - a long climb. North of Calvine the route is on the old A9, mostly closed to cars

Falls of Bruar are a short walk from the nearby tea room and tourist shop

attractive tea room in the old water-mill in Blair Atholl, home baking with locally milled produce. Visit Blair Castle (see text)

at this junction access between Pitlochry and the B8019 (B8079) is by passing under the main A9

go through Pitlochry on the main st (Atholl Road)

cross the River Tay on the A827 *bridge footway* to keep off the A827

follow signs to the suspension bridge over the River Tummel (walk) and Pitlochry Festival Theatre

cross the River Tay on old Logierait railway bridge (not visible). *South Side* track beside stone cottage

road to Pitlochry is signed Dunfallandy at Logierait

River Garry

Calvine

B847

Bruar Water

Bruar

B8079

A9

Tummel Forest

Loch Tummel

B8019

Blair Atloll

River Tummell

B8079

A9

N

W   E

S

Pitlochry

Grandtully

minor road

River Tay

A827

A827

minor road

A924

7

B898

Logierait

B898

Ballinluig

A9

1 mile

GRANDTULLY TO CALVINE

Grandtully and Calvine are nothing much but between them lies the town of Pitlochry. Pitlochry seems at first glance to be a seaside resort marooned in the middle of the Highlands, but look more closely – it has plenty of charms. The pub at Moulin is worth a visit and there's lots of peaceful walks by the River Tummel for the evening. There is of course everything you might need including an excellent youth hostel, a camp site and a good bike shop.

South of Pitlochry you have to cross the River Tay on the Old Logierait railway bridge. This is easily missed from either direction – read the instructions on the map and look for it. The minor road between Logierait and Pitlochry has quite a lot of ups and downs. There is a hotel in Logierait.

Between Pitlochry and Blair Atholl you're rolling along on the B8019 / B8079, and it should be fairly quiet though cars can be fast moving. Blair Atholl village is quite small but the restored water mill is worth visiting, both for the tea room and to look at the machinery.

There's lots to see inside Blair Castle, home of the Duke of Atholl, and there's a lot outside too. Blair Castle is home to the Atholl Highlanders, supposedly the only private army allowed in Britain. Entry to the grounds is free for bikes so it's a good place to have your picnic; there are a few giant redwoods in the woods but they haven't yet reached the size of those in California.

North of Blair Atholl the route starts out prettily but the countryside slowly becomes bleaker as the road begins its long climb towards the Pass of Drumochter. There's a new tourist shop and tea room at Bruar but the short walk to the Falls of Bruar is still attractive. Bruar is the last place to eat before your climb over Drumochter so make sure you've got enough calories.

Beyond Calvine and nearby Struan the route is along the old road which is now used as the cycle route. Access for cars is preserved for those few people whose houses are actually on the road.

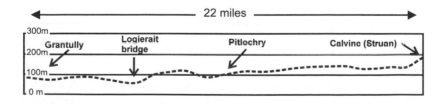

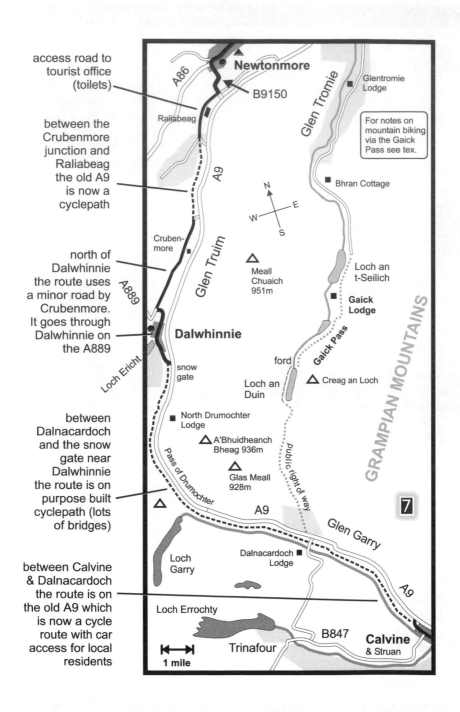

access road to tourist office (toilets)

between the Crubenmore junction and Raliabeag the old A9 is now a cyclepath

north of Dalwhinnie the route uses a minor road by Crubenmore. It goes through Dalwhinnie on the A889

between Dalnacardoch and the snow gate near Dalwhinnie the route is on purpose built cyclepath (lots of bridges)

between Calvine & Dalnacardoch the route is on the old A9 which is now a cycle route with car access for local residents

A86

Newtonmore

B9150

Glen Tromie

Glentromie Lodge

Raliabeag

A9

For notes on mountain biking via the Gaick Pass see tex.

Bhran Cottage

N
W   E
S

Cruben-more

Glen Truim

Meall Chuaich 951m

Loch an t-Seilich

A889

Dalwhinnie

Gaick Lodge

Loch Ericht

ford

Gaick Pass

GRAMPIAN MOUNTAINS

snow gate

Loch an Duin

Creag an Loch

North Drumochter Lodge

A'Bhuidheanch Bheag 936m

Glas Meall 928m

Pass of Drumochter

public right of way

7

A9

Glen Garry

Loch Garry

Dalnacardoch Lodge

A9

Loch Errochty

B847

Calvine
& Struan

1 mile

Trinafour

CALVINE TO NEWTONMORE

Going north this is a long well-graded climb to Dalwhinnie. Between Calvine and Dalnacardoch the route uses the old road. North of Dalnacardoch to the snow gate at Dalwhinnie a cyclepath has recently been completed. Previously you had to mix it with traffic moving at 70mph or more; unsurprisingly few did.

The line the route takes was established by General Wade when he was building roads after Prince Charlie's '45 rebellion, but it's not the only way you can go. You might wonder why General Wade did not use the Gaick, rather than the Pass of Drumochter, when planning his route north. It's the same elevation and more direct. Possibly the reason was the threat of winter avalanches on the steeper slopes of the Gaick.

Road and rail engineers continued with the Wade line so the A9, the railway, and the new cyclepath sweep to the west, leaving the Gaick to the occasional walker and mountain biker. It is possible for cycle tourers to use the Gaick but you will need to walk some sections.

At the south end the start of the Gaick route is opposite the road junction for Trinafour, marked 'Public Footpath by Gaick to Speyside'. Between there and Loch an Duin it's a rough track. Along the side of Loch an Duin it's a rough footpath; at the north end of Loch an Duin you have to wade across a river. After that it's rough track to Loch an t-Seilich, then a good tarmac estate road thereafter.

Don't attempt the Gaick route unless you have: reasonably dry weather (the river crossing would be dangerous otherwise); Sheet 42 OS Landranger Map; plenty of food (the water out of the burns is OK); warm waterproof clothing. You could do it as a circular too.

Dalwhinnie has a hotel, a café, a shop, a train station, and a distillery. Between there and Crubenmore it's a back road with good views, then between Crubenmore and Raliabeag the old A9 has been used as a cyclepath again. At Raliabeag you go past a tourist office and a car park and use the B9150 leading to Newtonmore.

Newtonmore is a quiet village with tea rooms, several food shops, B&Bs, a good pub and quite a pleasant independent hostel.

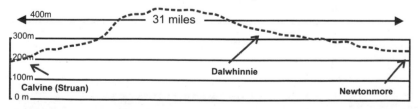

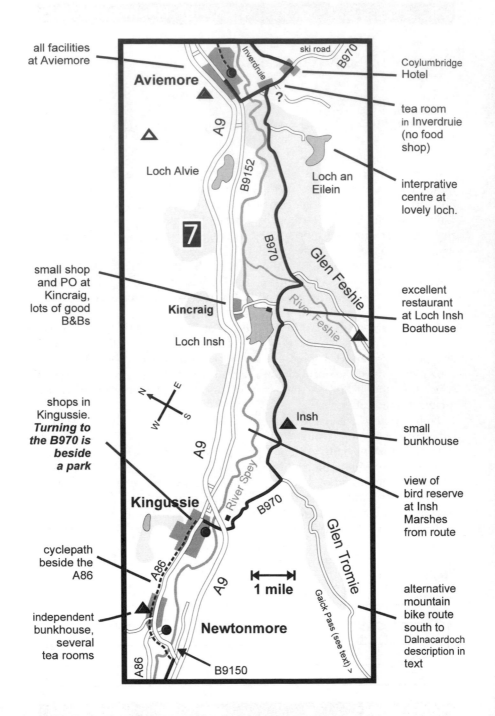

all facilities at Aviemore

Aviemore

Inverdruie

ski road

B970

Coylumbridge Hotel

tea room in Inverdruie (no food shop)

?

A9

B9152

Loch Alvie

Loch an Eilein

interprative centre at lovely loch.

B970

Glen Feshie

7

small shop and PO at Kincraig, lots of good B&Bs

Kincraig

River Feshie

excellent restaurant at Loch Insh Boathouse

Loch Insh

N
E
S
W

shops in Kingussie. *Turning to the B970 is beside a park*

A9

Insh

small bunkhouse

River Spey

B970

view of bird reserve at Insh Marshes from route

Kingussie

cyclepath beside the A86

A86

1 mile

A9

Glen Tromie

alternative mountain bike route south to Dalnacardoch description in text

independent bunkhouse, several tea rooms

A86

Newtonmore

Gaick Pass (see text) >

B9150

NEWTONMORE TO AVIEMORE

There is some lovely country between Newtonmore and Aviemore, with Caledonian pine woods, and the backdrop of the Cairngorm and Monadhliath mountains. It's a popular holiday area but the back roads are mostly quiet. Glen Feshie is particularly attractive and worth a diversion; the road on the west side has the best views.

Between Newtonmore and Kingussie the route runs on a cyclepath beside the A86; the A86 isn't particularly busy. Kingussie has an independent hostel, lots of B&Bs and hotels, pubs, restaurants, a bike shop, a train station and a good supermarket.

There's an attractive public park with picnic tables in Kingussie; this is where the route turns off the A86 to the train station, using the B970 via Insh to Inverdruie near Aviemore. The B970 is a lovely little road, quite quiet with beautiful views.

The route south via the Gaick starts at Tromie Bridge three miles north of Kingussie. This is a small stone bridge with a wide turning circle for timber lorries to get round on one side. Cunningly, in order to convince people that the Glen Tromie road doesn't go anywhere much, the estate have left the first 300m or so unsurfaced.

There's a small bunkhouse at Insh but no source of food so if you stay there remember to get your groceries first. Further north again there is an excellent restaurant 100m off the route at the boathouse by Loch Insh. You can stay there too, they have a variety of types of accommodation and there are also several excellent B&Bs around Kincraig, plus a small post office and shop.

At Inverdruie there are outdoor equipment shops, a good café, Rothiemurchus Visitor Centre and a mountain bike hire shop. I have put a question mark on the map here because if you are going north a decision is required (see next page).

Aviemore has most amenities including a youth hostel, tourist information, ski shops, supermarkets, Burger King, swimming pool and ice rink, but architecturally it's not particularly attractive; they are supposed to be doing something about that. There's a good youth hostel and forest camp site five miles away, up the ski road at Glenmore.

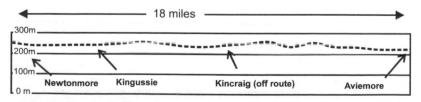

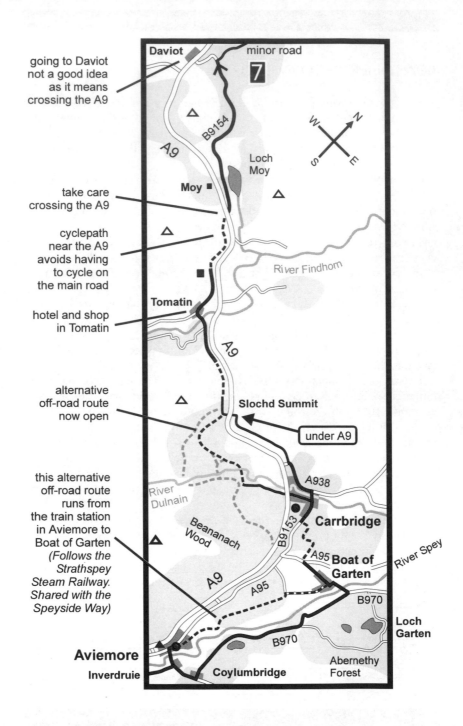

going to Daviot not a good idea as it means crossing the A9

take care crossing the A9

cyclepath near the A9 avoids having to cycle on the main road

hotel and shop in Tomatin

alternative off-road route now open

this alternative off-road route runs from the train station in Aviemore to Boat of Garten *(Follows the Strathspey Steam Railway. Shared with the Speyside Way)*

Daviot

minor road

7

Loch Moy

Moy ■

River Findhorn

Tomatin

A9

A9

Slochd Summit

under A9

A938

River Dulnain

Beananach Wood

B9153

Carrbridge

A95

Boat of Garten

River Spey

A9

A95

B970

Loch Garten

Aviemore

Inverdruie

Coylumbridge

B970

Abernethy Forest

B9154

AVIEMORE TO ROAD JUNCTION NEAR DAVIOT

Between Boat of Garten and Aviemore you can go beside the Strathspey Steam Railway or use the B970. The rail route is shared with the Speyside Way extension and the shared part will be signed as a bike route. You can cycle much of it anyway, though fragile parts have to be cycled on back roads. It comes out at Spey Bay (see page 122).

The B970 is quiet and bonny with views through the forest to the Cairngorms; the River Spey runs close by. Boat of Garten is a station on the steam railway, where there are shops and a pub. A worthwhile diversion is to Loch Garten, a nature reserve in the Caledonian pine forest from where ospreys were reintroduced to the Highlands. The fish farm at Aviemore gave them a good start.

Between Carrbridge and Boat of Garten there's a forest route avoiding the A95: again this will be signposted. Carrbridge is noteable for the Landmark Centre which combines an elevated forest nature trail with a good bookshop and restaurant. There is a good pub too as well as a tourist office.

North of Carrbridge the route briefly follows the A938, which isn't particularly busy, then uses a section of old road to reach the Slochd Summit. After that it's cyclepath and a back road to Tomatin. Another off-road alternative is from Carrbridge too. This starts along the south bank of the River Dulnain near the old bridge at Carrbridge then joins an old General Wade road to travel north via historic Sluggan Bridge.

On the way to Tomatin the route crosses Findhorn Bridge. A lovely little road runs up the north bank of the River Findhorn from there and can eventually take you to Inverness via Farr, but I'd better stick to the subject of this book and not try to describe too many side diversions.

Near Tomatin Distillery the route becomes cyclepath again before crossing the A9 near Moy. There isn't very much at Moy; going north from there the route climbs gently though a forest then descends steeply towards the River Nairn. Going north don't go flying down the hill too fast as you have to make a right turn on to a minor road before you get to the bottom.

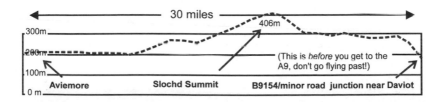

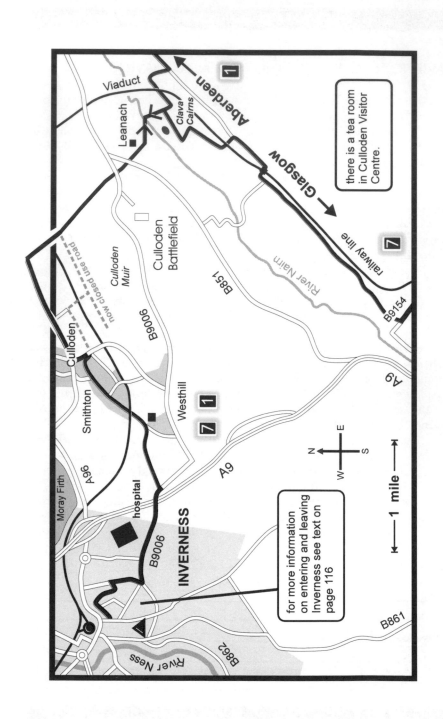

ROAD JUNCTION NEAR DAVIOT TO INVERNESS

Between the B9154 and Leanach the route runs high above the south bank of the River Nairn. It crosses the railway a couple of times, then at the Leanach end, dips down to cross the river. Just east of here is Culloden Battlefield and the associated visitor centre; access to it is just off the route from the B9006.

After its long retreat from Derby the half-starved, under-strength Highlanders had to face a disiplined Hanoverian army under the Duke of Cumberland. The charge of the clans failed to break the redcoats, sustained by their artillery and ranks of bayonets. A thousand of the Highland army died and Prince Charles Edward Stuart eventually escaped to France.

No such escape was possible for the Highland people though, and an example was made of them with the banning of Highland dress, burnings and summary arrests. The National Trust for Scotland describes all this vividly in the visitor centre which has a good bookshop and restaurant. The nearby Clava Cairns, Bronze Age burial chambers, are worth seeing.

Inverness is the great southern city to those living in Caithness and Sutherland but as towns go it's not particularly large. The Caledonian Canal terminates there and you can take a cruise from Inverness along Loch Ness to Urquhart Castle.

Cycling along by Loch Ness is possible too, as the Forestry Commission Great Glen Cycle Route (mountain biking) runs all the way to Fort William. If you want to road cycle go along the southern side of Loch Ness by Dores and Inverfarigaig; the A82 on the north side of Loch Ness is both narrow and very busy

Culturally Inverness has a lot to offer; Eden Court Theatre usually has something interesting on, and Celtic folk music and Celtic culture are continually being reinvented. If you are into Scottish fiddle music it would be worth investigating some of the pubs where there may well be live music.

There are several good bike shops, both independent and SYHA youth hostels, and lots of B&Bs and hotels. All the same if you are coming in the summer it's advisable to book in advance.

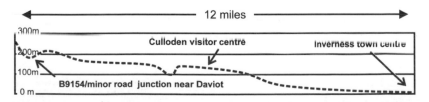

5

INVERNESS–JOHN O' GROATS

TOTAL DISTANCE – 170 MILES
FOR INVERNESS TO JOHN O' GROATS START AT PAGE 110
FOR JOHN O' GROATS TO INVERNESS START AT PAGE 115
  AND WORK BACKWARDS

INTRODUCTION

From Inverness there are two choices. The best is north through the Black Isle
via Cromarty and the Nigg ferry. The Nigg ferry is the only ferry from the
Black Isle, travelling between Cromarty and Nigg (tel: 01381 610269; mobile:
07768 653674; email: info@cromarty-ferry.co.uk). The ferry runs from May

to October from 8 a.m. to
6 p.m. approximately. Outside
the summer months it is not
possible to make the crossing
so a winter route is given. The
B9176 isn't used by the winter
route as it avoids Tain. It's
reasonably quiet but hilly, great
views though!

The Black Isle isn't quite an
island; the Cromarty, Moray
and Beauly Firths isolate it
from the rest of Scotland and
it used to be secret country
before the Beauly Firth was
bridged and the A9 driven
across from Inverness on the
Kessock Bridge.

Now the southern parts
have become popular with
commuters working in
Inverness but it's still fairly
quiet.

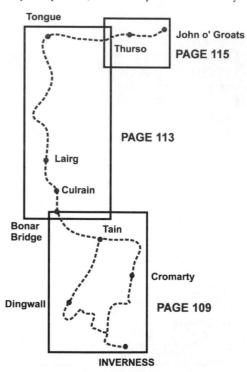

Cromarty, the ancient royal burgh at the northern tip, isn't much larger than a village but has a quiet charm.

Further north, Tain is a substantial small Victorian town; like Cromarty it has historical connections with Scandinavia.

After Bonar Bridge and Lairg, settlements are less frequent and it's advisable to make sure you have sufficient food with you to power your bike along the lonely single-track roads.

There are substantial mountains as you work north: Ben Kilbreck, Ben Loyal and Ben Hope, the most northerly of Scotland's Munros (mountains over 3,000 feet). You'll only see the odd hillwalker as this is too far north for most walkers to reach conveniently on a weekend.

The roads are sometimes subject to a 'rush hour' between 4 p.m. and 5 p.m., but we're talking about perhaps three cars together here. Even the class A roads are single track with passing places. The locals can get annoyed if they are held up by inconsiderate behaviour, so if there isn't room for them to squeeze conveniently past, pull in. It's advisable to do this for lorries anyway.

You'll notice from the maps that here the word 'glen' is less frequent, being replaced by 'strath'. Strath means 'broad mountain valley', and here you'll notice the hills are not closely packed together but separated by wide sweeping valleys. The name is also used in Scottish country dancing, the Strathspey being literally a dance from the valley of the Spey.

The north coast of Scotland is a remote place, confronting the turbulent waters of the Pentland Firth and Atlantic. The steep cliffs are broken here and there by solitary beaches and by long fingers of the sea, the Kyle of Tongue for example. The road twists and turns but as it approaches Thurso and John o' Groats there is gentler country and the going gets easier. This is the Flow Country: half water, half land and all bog. It has a unique community of birds and animals. There is a RSPB visitor centre near the railway station at Forsinard.

The triangle between Thurso, John o' Groats and Wick has a lot of farmland and this area is more populated. Thurso has most things including a bike shop and a Nuclear Power Development Establishment at nearby Dounreay. This has had bad press in recent years.

There's not much to say about John o' Groats – going there is the point. There's a foot passenger ferry to Orkney and a car ferry from Scrabster. If you are going to Orkney go out on one and come back on the other. The Sustrans National Cycle Network extends to Orkney; there isn't space to cover Orkney here, but like most Scottish islands the cost of taking cars over on the ferry deters many people (the cost of petrol deters the locals), so the roads are reasonably quiet.

If this is your first cycle tour in Scotland, remember you've hardly scratched the surface – come back again.

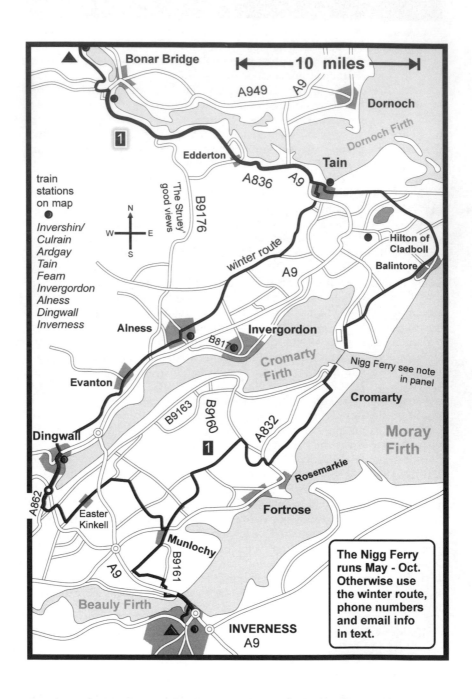

Bonar Bridge

10 miles

A949

A9

Dornoch

1

Dornoch Firth

Edderton

A836

A9

Tain

train
stations
on map

●

Invershin/
Culrain
Ardgay
Tain
Fearn
Invergordon
Alness
Dingwall
Inverness

'The Struey'
good views

B9176

N

W   E

S

winter route

A9

Hilton of
Cladboll

Balintore

Alness

B817

Invergordon

Cromarty
Firth

Nigg Ferry see note
in panel

Evanton

Cromarty

Dingwall

B9163

B9160

A832

Moray
Firth

A862

1

Easter
Kinkell

Rosemarkie

Fortrose

Munlochy

B9161

A9

Beauly Firth

INVERNESS
A9

The Nigg Ferry
runs May - Oct.
Otherwise use
the winter route,
phone numbers
and email info
in text.

INVERNESS TO BONAR BRIDGE

Several bridges cross the River Ness, but the one you need to use for going north is the Kessock Bridge over the Beauly Firth. It has a cyclepath. The River Ness runs through the middle of Inverness; find that then go downstream on the south bank of the river, depending on where you are it will go via: Castle Road; Bank Street; cyclepath under two bridges; Shore Street; Cromwell Road; Longman Drive; then direct access to the cyclepath on the bridge. The tourist office is just off Castle Road in Castle Wynd.

Going south to Inverness make sure you get off the bridge before the big roundabout on the south side, again keep by the water.

North of the Kessock Bridge the route leaves the A9 and passes through the village of North Kessock (shop and pub). After North Kessock you cross the A9 again, there is a short link, then you're on minor roads to Munlochy (shop and pub there too). Note: this area is being developed so the route may change.

There are two routes between Munlochy and Tain: the inland one via Dingwall, and the Black Isle route via Cromarty and the Nigg ferry (see page 108). Dingwall is a pleasant town but overall the Cromarty route is more attractive. You might have to go the other way if it's not summer as the ferry has less sailings. During the summer make sure you're visible on the pier.

Cromarty contains some of the most beautiful eighteenth-century buildings in Scotland. The history of the town is explained in Cromarty Courthouse. North of the Nigg ferry the route runs past an oil rig fabrication yard, then turns east after a mile.

Balintore and Hilton of Cladboll are former fishing villages running together and there's a pub and a shop. Just south you pass a Pictish symbol stone protected by a giant glass case.

Tain is a solid town of Sandstone; there's a good tea room in the High Street. West of Tain you have to cycle on the A9 as far as the bridge over the Dornoch Firth, then the traffic gets less. By all means go into Bonar Bridge but remember the route doesn't – it turns off at Ardgay on the west side of the Kyle of Sutherland. Possibly you'll be heading for the Gothic pile known as Carbisdale Castle Youth Hostel.

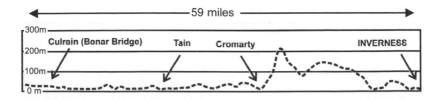

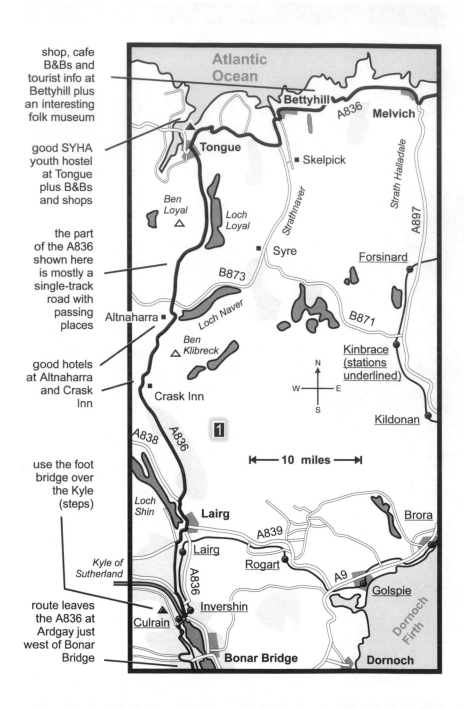

shop, cafe B&Bs and tourist info at Bettyhill plus an interesting folk museum

good SYHA youth hostel at Tongue plus B&Bs and shops

the part of the A836 shown here is mostly a single-track road with passing places

good hotels at Altnaharra and Crask Inn

use the foot bridge over the Kyle (steps)

route leaves the A836 at Ardgay just west of Bonar Bridge

Atlantic Ocean

Bettyhill

A836

Melvich

Tongue

Skelpick

Ben Loyal

Loch Loyal

Strathnaver

Strath Halladale

A897

Syre

Forsinard

B873

B871

Altnaharra

Loch Naver

Ben Klibreck

Kinbrace (stations underlined)

N
W   E
S

Crask Inn

Kildonan

A838

A836

1

10 miles

Loch Shin

Lairg

Lairg

A839

Brora

Kyle of Sutherland

Rogart

A9

A836

Culrain

Invershin

Golspie

Dornoch Firth

Bonar Bridge

Dornoch

BONAR BRIDGE TO MELVICH

Culrain might be wee but there are two train stations close by, Culrain and Invershin, the other side of the Kyle of Sutherland. There wasn't any way for people to get over other than on the train, hence the need for two stations. Flag the train down, incidentally.

Once there were dire warnings in Carbisdale Castle Youth Hostel telling cyclists not use the rail bridge. This saved you an eight-mile diversion via Bonar Bridge going north, so not a few risked the wrath of British Rail and sneaked over. Now there's a footbridge; it's not worth risking your life just to avoid a few steps.

Carbisdale is the flagship of the SYHA and was built as part of the divorce settlement of the Duchess of Sutherland. During the Second World War the King of Norway lived there. They do meals.

Further north eating places are far apart but you can get food at the Crask Inn and Altnaharra; the hotels around here cater mostly for fishermen but they'll serve cyclists too. Ben Loyal is a fine-looking mountain with a jagged ridge; the road runs right by Loch Loyal with the mountain climbing steeply above.

Tongue has a youth hostel in a big old house, shops, a camp site and a hotel. The village is strung out along the steep hillside overlooking the Kyle of Tongue so your bike might be handy.

There are more tourist facilities at Bettyhill on the coast further east, which include a tourist office and the Strathnaver Museum which has displays about the Clearances. Bettyhill was in fact established as a village for evicted crofters, cleared off the land in favour of sheep which were more profitable.

The clan chiefs who the crofters might have looked to for protection from the Clearances were by now seduced by the consumer society. Crofts were set on fire so people could not return to them; an eyewitness in 1819 counted 250 crofts put to the torch in one night.

A famous item in the churchyard at Bettyhill is the Farr Stone. This intricately carved cross dates from the ninth century and is still in fine condition as the artist was working in hard schist.

There are toilets at Melvich and a hostelry, but no shop.

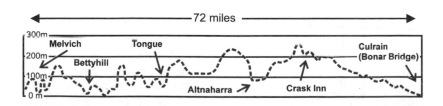

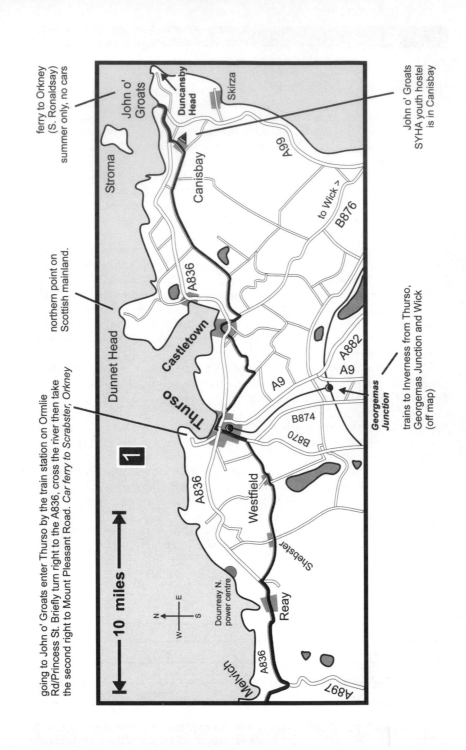

going to John o' Groats enter Thurso by the train station on Ormlie Rd/Princess St. Briefly turn right to the A836, cross the river then take the second right to Mount Pleasant Road. *Car ferry to Scrabster, Orkney*

10 miles

N
W — E
S

1

northern point on Scottish mainland.

Dunnet Head

ferry to Orkney (S. Ronaldsay) summer only, no cars

John o' Groats

Stroma

Duncansby Head

Skirza

Canisbay

A99

to Wick >

B876

John o' Groats SYHA youth hostel is in Canisbay

Castletown

A836

Thurso

A836

A9

A882

A9

Georgemas Junction

B874

B870

trains to Inverness from Thurso, Georgemas Junction and Wick (off map)

Westfield

Shebster

Dounreay N. power centre

Reay

Melvich

A836

A897

MELVICH TO JOHN O' GROATS

Going east there's a climb out of Melvich but after that it becomes easier. When you approach Thurso the twists and turns are over. There will be more local traffic on the roads by now.

Thurso was Scotland's most important port for trading with Scandinavia; it's still the largest town on the mainland north of Inverness. The Fast Breeder Nuclear Reactor at nearby Dounreay was at one time the great hope of the nuclear industry and it boosted employment in the town. This has faded now but it seems likely that it will continue to provide employment for some time as it will take 20 years or more to close the site down safely.

Much of Thurso was planned by Sir John Sinclair in the eighteenth century. The Thurso Folk Museum is interesting (open summer only and closes for lunch), and there is a bike shop. Scrabster just to the north is the terminal for the ferry to Orkney. This is the car ferry but it does sail past the dramatic cliffs of Hoy, including the famous rock stack, The Old Man of Hoy. Not surprisingly the country between Thurso and John o' Groats is quite similar to that of the Mainland of Orkney (the main island is called Mainland). If you are going there you can catch a foot passenger ferry from John o' Groats.

John o' Groats is an odd place for tourists to go; there is a hotel, a tourist office and a few gift shops. It is often regarded as the opposite point on the British mainland from Land's End in Cornwall. Jan de Groot was a Dutchman who James IV employed to start a ferry to the recently acquired Orkney Islands. He is said to have built an octagonal house to solve squabbles in the family about precedence, and the hotel has an octagonal tower in his memory.

John o' Groats is not actually the most northerly point of mainland Scotland however, that's Dunnet Head. Duncansby Head, a mile east of John o' Groats is the true north-east tip of Scotland so you will just have to go there won't you! The cliffs are alive with sea birds, there's a lighthouse – more interesting than John o' Groats itself.

If you need transport south from here with a bike the train is the only way to go. There's a station in Thurso but it may be easier to pick it up at Georgemas Junction. In summer there are special arrangements for carrying bicycles.

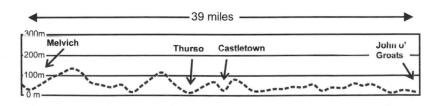

6

INVERNESS–ABERDEEN

TOTAL DISTANCE – 152 MILES
FOR INVERNESS TO ABERDEEN START AT PAGE 118
FOR ABERDEEN TO INVERNESS START AT PAGE 131
AND WORK BACKWARDS

INTRODUCTION

Mostly this is a coastal route – the sea is never very far away and you pass though fishing villages such as Cullen, and interesting small towns like Elgin and Banff. It's similar to Cornwall in many ways – all that's missing is the crowds. The area is popular with golfers and the Whisky Trail is not far away. Mostly it's the Scots who have discovered it. There are lots of quiet rural roads – a great area for cycling!

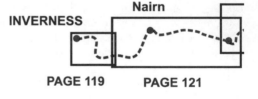

Doing Inverness to Aberdeen, the wind is more likely to be at your back. The railway line between Aberdeen and Inverness is reasonably near much of the time so hopping on a train with your bike is a reasonable option.

There are a number of historic places to visit, Culloden Battlefield of course, and just east of this is Cawdor Castle, a fascinating place which deserves at least half a day. There are other castles too; Brodie Castle with its well landscaped grounds is very near to the route.

The route skirts the Grampian Mountains so isn't particularly hilly. It passes through some attractive woodland at times and even the plantation forests are mostly Scots pine instead of Sitka spruce – Scots pine being more suited to the sandy soil.

Travelling along the coast, views of the sea are mixed with coastal forests. A long relaxed section is by Culbin Forest just west of Findhorn, which is now a nature reserve. Further west still there is interesting cliff scenery near Cullen. Most of the tea rooms in Cullen serve Cullen Skink, the local fish soup. Nowadays you can also get it in Fochabers, though that's the tinned variety, produced by Baxters.

Between Banff and Aberdeen the route cuts inland, running through farming country. When I first cycled there about six years ago with a Spokes cycling group I expected it to be a bit ordinary – far from it, the countryside is really pretty and surprisingly quiet.

As you approach Aberdeen of course it becomes busier. The route is less satisfactory between Dyce and Aberdeen, and less experienced cyclists might prefer to catch a train to avoid busy roads and sightsee in Aberdeen on foot.

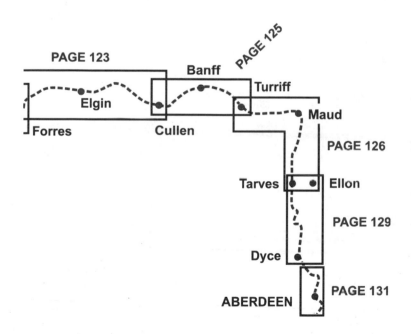

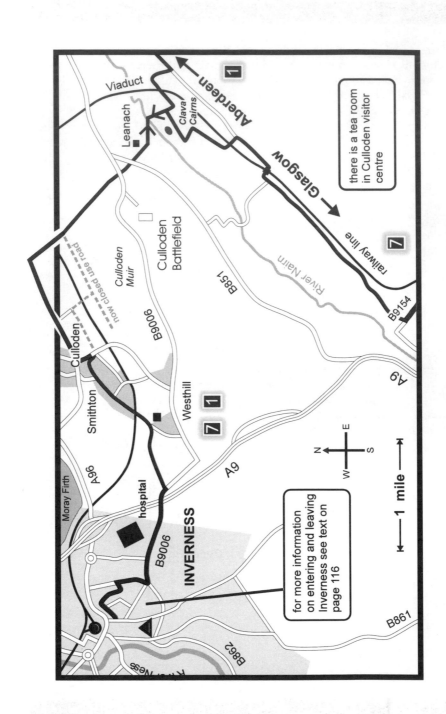

INVERNESS TO CULLODEN BATTLEFIELD

Some basic information about Inverness is given at the end of the Glasgow to Inverness chapter.

From Inverness the most important thing is to cross the A9 dual carriageway on the B9006. This runs immediately south of the main Raigmore Hospital so it is not difficult to find.

Entering Inverness after crossing the A9 continue straight on past the hospital to enter Culcabock Road. Turn right into Kingsmills Road which leads to the pedestrian precinct in the centre of town. Tourist information is at the far (north) end near the castle.

Leaving Inverness from the south end of the pedestrian precinct you go via: Crown Road, Crown Drive, right into Direbught Road, left to Culcabock Road and continue on to cross the dual carriageway. After crossing turn left to a minor road.

Shortly after leaving Inverness you pass by the village of Culloden then pass near Culloden Battlefield, which is off the B9006.

After its long retreat from Derby the under-strength Highlanders had to face a disiplined Hanoverian army under the Duke of Cumberland. This time the charge of the clans failed. Over 1000 of the Highland army died and Prince Charles Edward Stuart eventually escaped to France.

No such escape was possible for the Highland people though, and an example was made of them. The National Trust for Scotland describes all this vividly in the visitor centre which has a good bookshop and restaurant.

After passing through Leanach the route divides. For Aberdeen etc, drop down to the River Nairn and then go under the railway viaduct.

A few miles east of here (map on next page) is Cawdor Castle. This is a joy to visit, the garden is wonderful and the castle itself is everything a castle should be, with many fascinating and eccentric things inside.

There is a legend that the early Thane of Cawdor, wanting a new castle, had a dream that he was to load a donkey with gold and let it wander until it lay down and chose the site. He did this and the donkey lay down by a thorn tree. There is still a tree within the castle. The castle, incidentally, is the one mentioned in Shakespeare's play *Macbeth*.

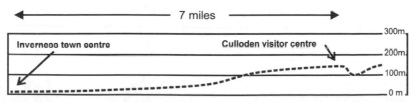

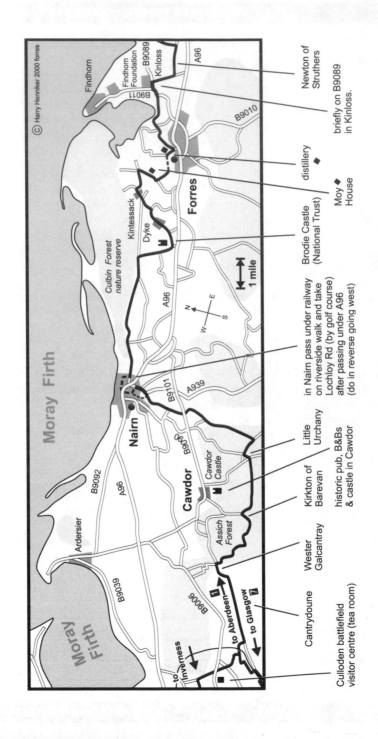

© Harry Henniker 2000 forres

Moray Firth

Moray Firth

Findhorn

Findhorn Foundation

B9011

Kinloss

B9089

A96

Culbin Forest nature reserve

Kintessack

Dyke

Forres

B9010

N
W — E
S

1 mile

A96

Ardersier

B9092

A96

Nairn

B9101

A939

B9090

Cawdor

Cawdor Castle

Assich Forest

B9039

B9006

to Inverness

to Aberdeen 1

to Glasgow 7

Newton of Struthers

briefly on B9089 in Kinloss.

distillery

Moy ◆ House

Brodie Castle (National Trust)

in Nairn pass under railway on riverside walk and take Lochloy Rd (by golf course after passing under A96 (do in reverse going west)

Little Urchany

Kirkton of Barevan

historic pub, B&Bs & castle in Cawdor

Wester Galcantray

Cantrydoune

Culloden battlefield visitor centre (tea room)

CULLODEN BATTLEFIELD TO FORRES

Cawdor is an interesting old village with B&Bs and an old pub. The route here is in wooded country with short steep hills where the roads cross rivers. Towards Nairn the country is flatter. Nairn is a small seaside resort with a sandy beach, lots of B&Bs, a bike shop and a tourist office.

After Nairn the route runs along the coast by Culbin Forest. This is flat and you bowl along quite easily if there's no head wind. Culbin Forest was at one time known as the Scottish Sahara. Establishing the forest was a triumph for the Forestry Commission. There's no place to get food between Nairn and Forres unless you go to Brodie Castle.

Brodie Castle is run by the National Trust for Scotland, though the Brodies still live there and have done since 1567. You can rely on the National Trust to have good tea rooms. The gardens are open all year and are lovely, with daffodils in the spring. The castle has lots of interesting rooms and was originally a Z plan but has had later additions.

Between Brodie Castle and Forres the route becomes more complex as you take to lanes to avoid the A96, but it should be well signposted. Forres is full of flower beds. The route doesn't enter Forres town, it hovers on the other side of the A96; the access point is by a distillery. It was raining when we were there and we all piled into a café which was very welcoming. The town would be attractive even without the flower beds.

Just north of Forres is Findhorn and the Findhorn Foundation, dedicated to a spiritually based, holistic planetary culture. I've several friends who have been there, but I'm still not entirely sure what it means – perhaps I'll go one day and find out. I'm sure Sustrans would have liked to put it on the route but you'll have to divert a couple of miles if you want to visit. There are sandy beaches at Findhorn but Findhorn Bay is muddy.

Kinloss has a pub and shops and is next to the RAF station of the same name. Nowadays it's a base for search and rescue helicopters operating over the North Sea and the Grampian and Cairngorm Mountains.

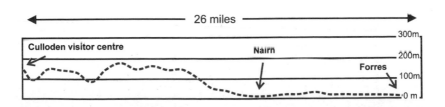

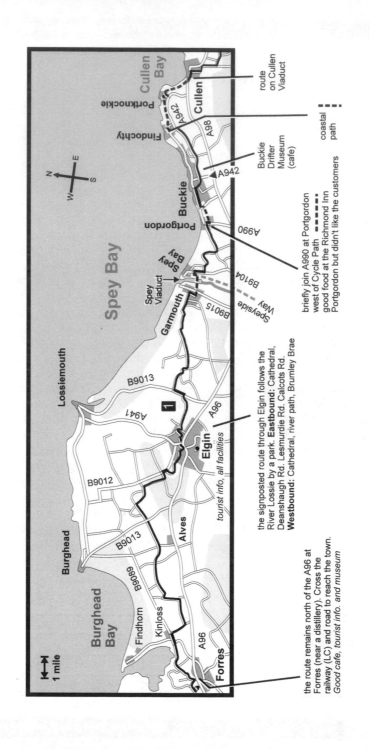

1 mile

W N E S

Burghead Bay

Burghead

Findhorn

Kinloss

Forres

A96

B9089

B9013

Alves

B9012

Lossiemouth

B9013

A941

Elgin
tourist info, all facilities

1

A96

Garmouth

Spey Bay

Spey Viaduct

Speyside Way

Spey Bay

B9015

B9104

Portgordon

A990

Buckie

A942

Findochty

Portknockie

A942

Cullen Bay

A98

Cullen

route on Cullen Viaduct

Buckie Drifter Museum (cafe)

coastal path

briefly join A990 at Portgordon
west of Cycle Path
good food at the Richmond Inn
Portgordon but didn't like the customers

the signposted route through Elgin follows the
River Lossie by a park. **Eastbound**: Cathedral,
Deanshaugh Rd. Lesmurdie Rd. Calcots Rd.
Westbound: Cathedral, river path, Brumley Brae

the route remains north of the A96 at
Forres (near a distillery). Cross the
railway (LC) and road to reach the town.
Good cafe, tourist info. and museum

FORRES TO CULLEN

From Forres the route is along quiet minor roads, then it joins the B9012 before entering Elgin. Elgin is a royal burgh and knows it still. It's the market town for the lands of Moray, and has a good park, lots of shops (bike shop), a museum, a tourist office, B&Bs and several hotels.

Despite all this Elgin isn't what it once was, the cathedral city of the north rivalling St Andrews. Elgin Cathedral is a magnificent ruin, though, and in the middle stands a Pictish cross slab, older than the cathedral. Elgin's a lively place and a good stopping point on your way east or west.

East of Elgin the route is near the sea with coastal views as you roll along to or from Garmouth. There's a cyclepath at Garmouth, over the River Spey to Spey Bay on the old Spey railway viaduct. Entry is by picnic tables at the south of the village off the B9015.

There's a hotel catering for golfers at Spey Bay, which is a hamlet as well as being the name of the bay itself. Near here is Tugnet Ice House, now a fishing museum. The nearby visitor centre and café is excellent.

Another route that starts here is the Speyside Way; it's not a cycle route but a long-distance walking route, but it has proved popular for cycling as much is on old railway and minor roads. The cycling differs slightly from the walking for environmental reasons but it follows the river all the way to Aviemore. If you're interested, get my other book, *101 Mountain Bike Routes in Scotland*.

Meanwhile we're on roads, through Portgordon, Buckie, Findochty and Portknockie (what splendid names). The route between Buckie and Portgordon is on the A990, a bit is on a path. The Buckie Drifter Museum is all about herring, and there's a steam drifter. It's worth a visit. I can't say the same about the restaurant as it took us ages to get served.

Again between Findochty and Portknockie you have to use an 'A' road, the A942 this time. After that though it's a great little path round sandy Cullen Bay. You'll also be able to ride over the impressive Cullen Viaduct.

Cullen is a wee stone town perched on a steep hillside. It's famous for Cullen Skink, a smoked haddock soup, which you can get it in all the cafés and tea rooms.

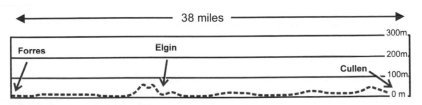

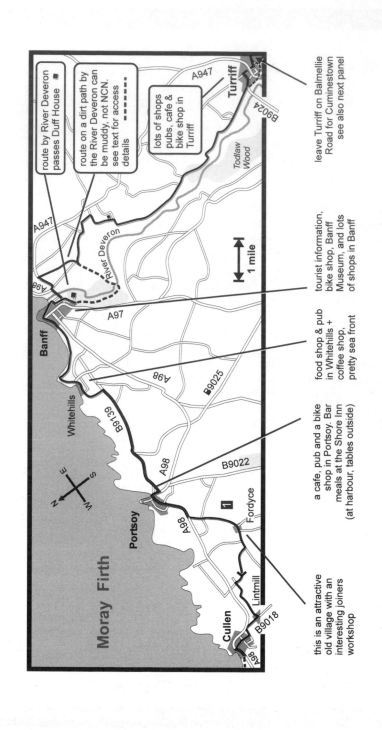

route by River Deveron passes Duff House ▮

route on a dirt path by the River Deveron can be muddy, not NCN. see text for access details

lots of shops pubs, cafe & bike shop in Turriff

A947

A947

Turriff

B9024

Todlaw Wood

leave Turriff on Balmellie Road for Cuminestown see also next panel

River Deveron

A98

Banff

A97

1 mile

tourist information, bike shop, Banff Museum, and lots of shops in Banff

Whitehills

A98

B9135

B9025

food shop & pub in Whitehills + coffee shop, pretty sea front

N
W   E
S

Portsoy

B9135

A98

B9022

a cafe, pub and a bike shop in Portsoy. Bar meals at the Shore Inn (at harbour, tables outside)

Fordyce

A98

1

Moray Firth

Cullen

Lintmill

B9018

A98

this is an attractive old village with an interesting joiners workshop

CULLEN TO TURRIFF

East of Cullen the route goes inland for a time, passing through Fordyce, a lovely old village with a joiner's workshop. East again is Portsoy which has an air of antiquity about it. This isn't surprising as some of the houses go back to the eighteenth century. Also famous is Portsoy marble; this even graces the palace at Versailles in the form of two fireplaces. Nowadays you can buy souvenirs made from it at the harbour: too heavy for cycling? Unlike Cullen, Portsoy has a bike shop.

If you like eighteenth-century architecture Banff will be your kind of place. The lairds from around here used to abandon their draughty castles in the winter and establish themselves in Banff for some socialising. The result was a number of substantial town houses. Banff harbour is silted up so it wouldn't be a fishing port even if there were any fish to catch.

If you are in this area for any time you may well hear comment about fishing quotas and arbitrary rules about who can fish for what and where. It might make one think that it was the civil servants applying the rules that had fished out the North Sea rather than the fishermen. Fishing still does go on, even if on a reduced scale compared to its heyday in the 1930s and '40s.

Depending on which way you go the route passes by Duff House, a great baroque mansion on the outskirts of Banff. This was in a bad state but has been restored and turned into an art gallery. William Adam started building Duff House in 1735. The building was for the first Earl of Fife but the parties disagreed and the whole thing turned into a legal battle.

The house was finished by the second earl without the help of William; nevertheless many features are designed by him – the facade ornamented with pilasters with Corinthian capitals and a lot of detailing. Inside there are some good Dutch seascapes and an El Greco.

Just south of Banff there is an interesting alternative way to go following the River Deveron (dotted line on map). It is a right of way for bikes and very pretty but is not signposted. Going south start at Duff House; going north follow a sign for Montcoffer.

Between Banff and Turriff it's a beautiful ride on a minor road by the River Deveron.

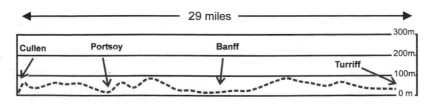

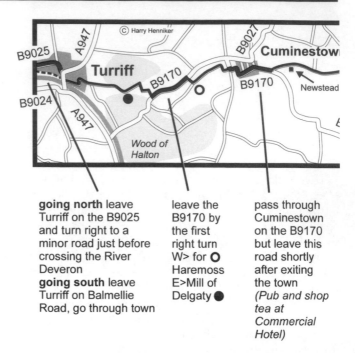

going north leave Turriff on the B9025 and turn right to a minor road just before crossing the River Deveron
going south leave Turriff on Balmellie Road, go through town

leave the B9170 by the first right turn W> for ○ Haremoss E>Mill of Delgaty ●

pass through Cuminestown on the B9170 but leave this road shortly after exiting the town *(Pub and shop tea at Commercial Hotel)*

TURRIFF TO TARVES OR ELLON

The country around here is very pretty too and there's no lack of facilities with bike shops in Turriff, Cuminestown and Ellon. The route uses the Formartine and Buchan Way, a long-distance route some of the time and you have the option of remaining on that between Auchnagatt and Ellon. If you do that though you'll miss out Haddo House (NTS), a rather splendid Adam-style mansion. What you'll also miss of course is a few hills, as the way passes along a former railway which naturally avoids them.

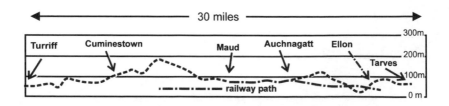

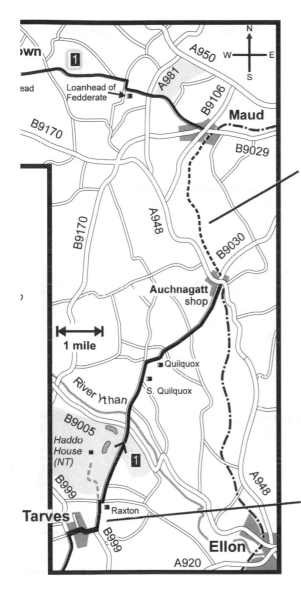

the route between Maud and Auchnagatt follows the Formartine and Buchan Way. In Maud the route is near the railway museum. You also have the option of following this long distance path between Dyce (Aberdeen Airport) and Auchnagatt. This is indicated on this and the next panel with a different dotted line symbol.

■—·■—·■—·■—·■—·■—·■—·■

shops pubs tea rooms in Maud, Auchnagatt and Ellon, plus a bike shop in Ellon.

route on road

route off-road

join B999 to pass through Tarves (*shops, hotel and post office*)

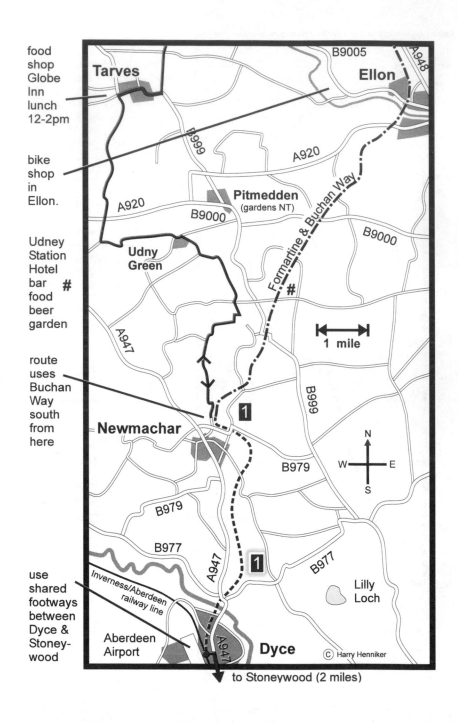

food
shop
Globe
Inn
lunch
12-2pm

Tarves

B9005

Ellon

A948

bike
shop
in
Ellon.

B999

A920

Pitmedden
(gardens NT)

A920

B9000

B9000

Formartine & Buchan Way

Udney
Station
Hotel
bar   **#**
food
beer
garden

**Udny
Green**

#

1 mile

A947

route
uses
Buchan
Way
south
from
here

1

Newmachar

B999

N

W   E

S

B979

B979

B977

A947

1

B977

Lilly
Loch

use
shared
footways
between
Dyce &
Stoney-
wood

Inverness/Aberdeen
railway line

A947

**Aberdeen
Airport**

Dyce

© Harry Henniker

to Stoneywood (2 miles)

TARVES OR ELLON TO DYCE

The roads start to become busier as we approach Aberdeen but the route will be quiet enough as far as Dyce. Whichever way you go, Pitmedden Garden is only a mile from the route and well worth sauntering round on a sunny day.

This is a seventeenth-century style formal garden, created by Sir Andrew Seton in the 1670s. It was rescued by the National Trust for Scotland and had to be largely re-created as it was, by 1950, mostly a kitchen garden.

This was done with a great deal of style. Seventeenth-century designs intended for the gardens at Holyrood Palace in Edinburgh were used. There's a maze of box hedges, masses of colourful annuals and all is peace and quiet. Quite a lot of the garden is sunken so you can appreciate the ornamental designs. There's also a small agricultural museum with an example of an Aberdeenshire farm worker's bothy (rough shelter).

Between Newmachar and Dyce the route is on the Formartine and Buchan Way again. If you are going south enjoy this because south of Dyce you will be next to heavy traffic on the A947 for two miles. This includes a very busy roundabout at Stoneywood to the south of Dyce. There are plans to improve this.

The route between Dyce and central Aberdeen is mostly on city streets and Sustrans suggests that you get the train between these two places if you have children with you. This is probably advisable, but when I cycled it last year with a friend we found it mostly fine and not too difficult to navigate – just pay attention to the street names (see map on next page). Dyce is also the location of Aberdeen airport.

Aberdeen is a much larger city than Inverness. The city is beside the river rather than by the beach, or one should say rivers, because it's both the River Don and the River Dee. This slight separation from the shore gives an open aspect to the city. Aberdeen is called the 'silver city' because of the granite of which it is built, but it's only silver on a sunny day. It has a reputation for being expensive owing to the oil industry but this mostly applies to house prices. There are lots of maritime connections even apart from the oil industry, and plenty of interesting museums and art galleries.

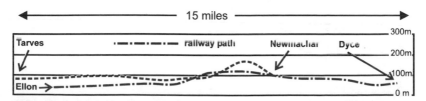

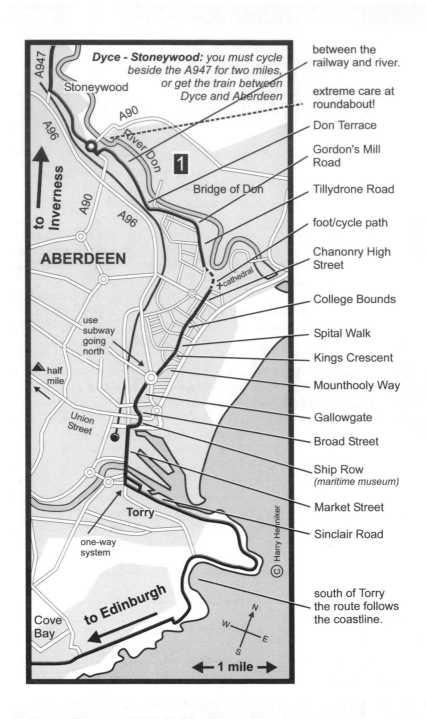

Dyce - Stoneywood: *you must cycle beside the A947 for two miles, or get the train between Dyce and Aberdeen*

A947

Stoneywood

A90

A96

River Don

1

between the railway and river.

extreme care at roundabout!

Don Terrace

Gordon's Mill Road

Tillydrone Road

foot/cycle path

Bridge of Don

to Inverness

A90

A96

Chanonry High Street

cathedral

ABERDEEN

College Bounds

Spital Walk

use subway going north

Kings Crescent

Mounthooly Way

half mile

Gallowgate

Broad Street

Union Street

Ship Row *(maritime museum)*

Market Street

Sinclair Road

Torry

one-way system

© Harry Henniker

south of Torry the route follows the coastline.

to Edinburgh

Cove Bay

N
W · E
S

← 1 mile →

DYCE TO ABERDEEN

As you can see from the map, at present only a small part of the route between Dyce and Stoneywood is on cyclepath. Aberdeen is said to be a mixture of St Andrews and Glasgow, having the atmosphere and seascapes of the latter but the planning mistakes of the former. Aberdeen also has excellent parks – for example, Duthie Park with its winter garden or Seaton Park near the cathedral.

St Machar's Cathedral is fifteenth century and is an interesting ruin; quite near is the university quarter and King's College, which was founded in 1495 and has a visitor centre. The cycle route, even if it is fairly busy, does pass by all of this.

Another aspect of Aberdeen that might be interesting is the docks; you can generally wander about the quays without anyone bothering you. There should be lots to look at: Kirkwall or Lerwick ferry boats coming and going (possibly you'll be catching one to cycle on Shetland?); sea-going barges laden with oil pipes; fishing boats; the fish market.

You can walk along the northern side of the docks to the tiny fishing village of Footdee at the very tip of Aberdeen harbour with the esplanade and Aberdeen beach stretching away into the distance – perhaps that's somewhere you could cycle more safely. Footdee is three little squares of cottages and is a self-contained community, quite surprising to come across so near to the big city.

Not too far away is the Maritime Museum (open Monday to Saturday) which is in another ancient building: Provost Ross's House. This traces Aberdeen's maritime history from the very beginning when the docks were being built, to the advent of the oil industry in a very comprehensive display.

Aberdeen has a tourist office in Broad Street (see map); the youth hostel is in Queens Road, slightly off the map. From central Aberdeen go along Union Street then fork right along Albyn Place to Queens Road, and the hostel is a little along on the right. Hotels in Aberdeen can be expensive due to the oil industry but there is still plenty of economical accommodation to be found (see Appendix).

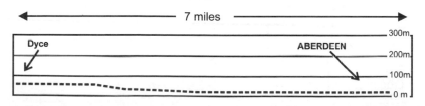

7

ABERDEEN–EDINBURGH

TOTAL DISTANCE – 170 MILES
FOR ABERDEEN TO EDINBURGH START AT PAGE 134
FOR EDINBURGH TO ABERDEEN START AT PAGE 154
   AND WORK BACKWARDS

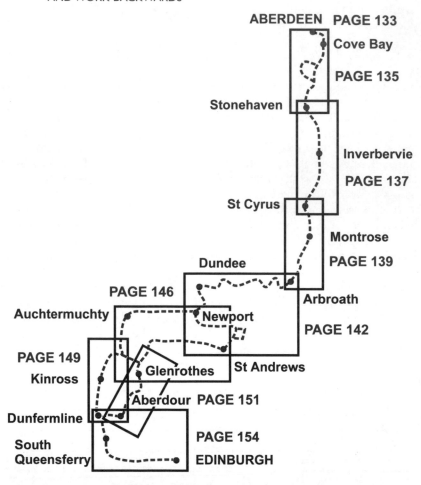

ABERDEEN **PAGE 133**
Cove Bay
PAGE 135
Stonehaven
Inverbervie
PAGE 137
St Cyrus
Montrose
PAGE 139
Dundee
Arbroath
PAGE 146
Auchtermuchty Newport
PAGE 142
PAGE 149
Kinross   Glenrothes   St Andrews
Aberdour **PAGE 151**
Dunfermline
South   **PAGE 154**
Queensferry   EDINBURGH

INTRODUCTION

Like the Inverness to Aberdeen route this has a maritime flavour, as it passes through east coast ports and fishing villages. South of this the route goes through Fife, known as the Kingdom of Fife, or simply The Kingdom.

Whether or not there ever was a king in Fife is lost in antiquity; the reason for the name was its relative isolation until recent times. This is gone now with the Forth Rail Bridge being opened over 100 years ago, and the Forth Road Bridge more recently. One of the best things about this route is cycling over the bridge.

Fife itself has its own network of cycle routes, 300 miles of them – the Kingdom of Fife Millennium Cycleways. The National Cycle Network makes much use of these to get north or south but they are well worth exploring on their own. The routes are marked on these pages but you can also get information from the project itself (address in Appendix).

The route passes through many famous places: Dunfermline with its abbey; Falkland with Falkland Palace; St Andrews, home of golf; Dundee, home of D C Thomson and the *Dandy* and *Beano* comics, not to mention the *Discovery*, the ship that took Captain Scott to the Antarctic, now returned to its birthplace.

North of this again are the fishing ports of Arbroath, Montrose and Inverbervie. You can still get Arbroath smokies in Arbroath but the fishing is much declined. There are also some beautiful beaches: Lunan Bay, where the cliffs south of Montrose are suddenly broken, is classically beautiful, and the beach north of St Andrews at Tentsmuir Forest is both long and remote-seeming, backed as it is by the forest.

There are some places where you have to mix with traffic: much has been done to improve this but some parts are not 'up to standard' as Sustrans says. There are more notes on Edinburgh in the Edinburgh to Glasgow chapter and Aberdeen in the Inverness to Aberdeen chapter.

ABERDEEN TO COVE BAY
(6 MILES, NOT HILLY)

For the map for this section see the Aberdeen map on p. 130. When leaving or entering Aberdeen you go through Torry and have to negotiate a one-way system there. South of that it's mostly a matter of staying by the sea between Aberdeen and Cove Bay.

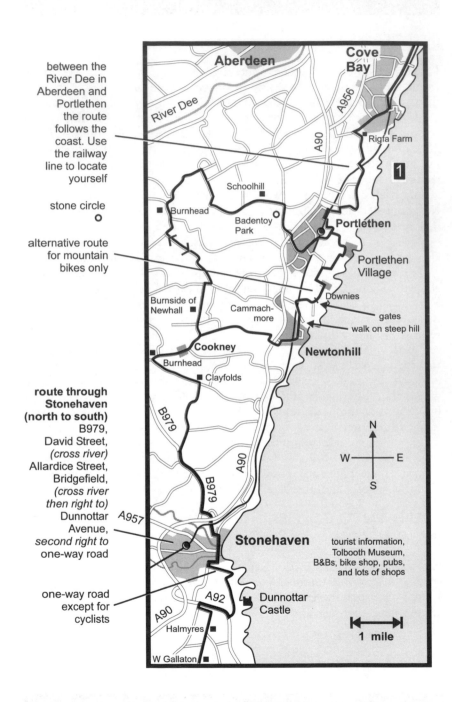

between the River Dee in Aberdeen and Portlethen the route follows the coast. Use the railway line to locate yourself

stone circle ○

alternative route for mountain bikes only

route through Stonehaven (north to south)
B979, David Street, *(cross river)* Allardice Street, Bridgefield, *(cross river then right to)* Dunnottar Avenue, *second right to* one-way road

one-way road except for cyclists

Aberdeen

Cove Bay

River Dee

A956

A90

Rigfa Farm

1

Schoolhill

Burnhead

Badentoy Park

Portlethen

Portlethen Village

Burnside of Newhall

Cammach-more

Downies

gates
walk on steep hill

Cookney

Burnhead

Clayfolds

Newtonhill

B979

A90

B979

N
W — E
S

A957

Stonehaven

tourist information, Tolbooth Museum, B&Bs, bike shop, pubs, and lots of shops

A90

A92

Dunnottar Castle

Halmyres

W Gallaton

⟵————⟶
1 mile

COVE BAY TO STONEHAVEN

There is a little navigation to do south of Cove Bay but if you remain east of the A92 as far as Portlethen you won't go far wrong. The railway line is often useful when orientating yourself.

Between Portlethen and Cookney you have the choice of going on a mountain bike route near the coast or travelling inland on roads. Unless you're a demon mountain-biker the longer inland route will be quicker even if it is longer. You can go either way on any bike of course, you'd just need to walk a bit more on a touring bike. The mountain bike route is not recommended if you have large amounts of luggage. The tiny harbours on the coast here are tucked into crannies in the cliffs.

> *SPECIAL NOTE: Between Aberdeen and Stonehaven Sustrans is currently investigating an alternative route using the pleasant and safe Deeside Railway Path to enter Aberdeen.

Stonehaven is more known as a seaside resort than a fishing port these days. It has a shingle beach; the oldest part is near the harbour, beyond that the Victorian town stretches up the hillside. It's a quiet sort of a place and a good stop on your way north or south. There's a tourist office.

The old sixteenth-century Tolbooth by the harbour is now a museum. At one time it was also a prison, then in 1748–9 Episcopal ministers lodged inside. They are said to have baptised children through the windows. Nowadays the Tolbooth has a very pleasant tea room next to the museum.

Stonehaven has a folk festival from 15–17 July, a three-day festival of contemporary and traditional music.

Dunnottar Castle immediately south of Stonehaven is just next to the route and you should certainly go there. It's on a 160-foot-high plug of rock by the coast. Seeing it, it's not surprising that it held out for so long during Cromwell's occupation.

During that time the Scottish regalia were sent there for safe-keeping as the Lord Protector might have melted them down. They were smuggled out again by the wife of the minister at Kineff and hidden under the pulpit at Kinneff Church (map next page) when the castle was occupied by Cromwell's troops. The crown and sceptre can be seen now in Edinburgh Castle.

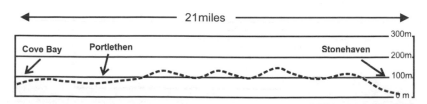

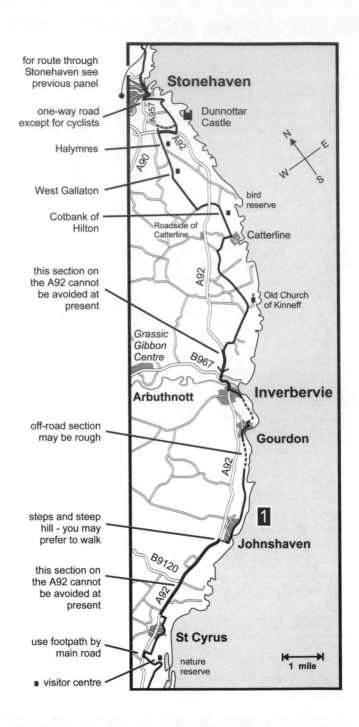

for route through Stonehaven see previous panel

Stonehaven

one-way road except for cyclists

Dunnottar Castle

Halymres

A957

A92

A90

West Gallaton

bird reserve

Cotbank of Hilton

Roadside of Catterline

Catterline

A92

this section on the A92 cannot be avoided at present

Old Church of Kinneff

Grassic Gibbon Centre

B967

Arbuthnott

Inverbervie

off-road section may be rough

Gourdon

A92

steps and steep hill - you may prefer to walk

1

Johnshaven

this section on the A92 cannot be avoided at present

B9120

A92

use footpath by main road

St Cyrus

nature reserve

■ visitor centre

N
W — E
S

1 mile

STONEHAVEN TO ST CYRUS

South of Dunnottar Castle the route is on minor roads, though with three short stretches on the A92 (take care). It crosses the A92 near Fowlsheugh Bird Colony (RSPB). There are over 100,000 nesting sea birds in the spring and summer breeding season, including kittiwakes, guillemots and razorbills. They can all be seen from the cliff tops but take care near the edge. There's an exhibition centre (no toilets).

South again is Catterline, where you should be able to get a cup of tea, and the Old Church of Kinneff where the Crown of Scotland was hidden under the church flagstones in 1651 by the local minister, Rev. James Grainger.

Inverbervie, nestling in Bervie Bay has B&Bs, shops and a café, but no bike shop. Inverbervie was spared by the Duke of Cumberland on his post-Culloden rampage because the local minister, entertained the Duke at the manse and persuaded him not to destroy the town.

The designer of the ship *Cutty Sark*, Hercules Linton, was born in Inverbervie. In 1969 Francis Chichester, the first single-handed circumnavigator of the world, unveiled a figurehead memorial in the town to him.

Slightly inland is the Grassic Gibbon Centre, for this is the Howe of the Mearns, difficult farming country made famous by James Leslie Mitchell in *Sunset Song*. He wrote under the pseudonym Lewis Grassic Gibbon. The centre gives some interesting background to the author's life and the surrounding country. There is a tea room.

Johnshaven derives its name of course from an earlier version, St John's Haven. It's an interesting little fishing village with an attractive harbour. It has connections with the Knights of the Hospital of St John of Jerusalem and it is from this that the name comes.

South of here again is St Cyrus Nature Reserve; there's a picnic area with toilets and many interesting plants and birds. The visitor centre has information about local history, natural history and salmon fishing. There's also a salt water aquarium. At present you have to cycle on the A92 for three miles between St Cyrus and Johnshaven; there are plans to improve this for cyclists.

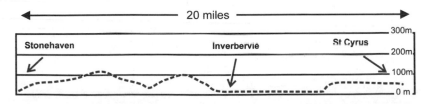

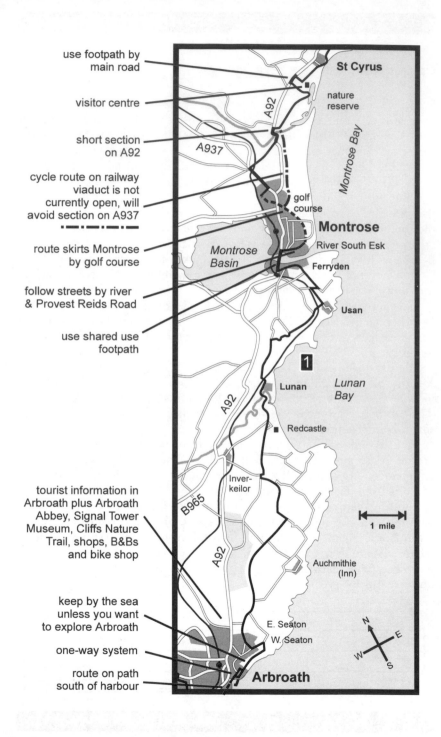

use footpath by main road

visitor centre

short section on A92

cycle route on railway viaduct is not currently open, will avoid section on A937

route skirts Montrose by golf course

follow streets by river & Provest Reids Road

use shared use footpath

tourist information in Arbroath plus Arbroath Abbey, Signal Tower Museum, Cliffs Nature Trail, shops, B&Bs and bike shop

keep by the sea unless you want to explore Arbroath

one-way system

route on path south of harbour

St Cyrus

nature reserve

A92

A937

Montrose Bay

golf course

Montrose

River South Esk

Montrose Basin

Ferryden

Usan

1

Lunan Bay

Lunan

Redcastle

Inver-keilor

B965

A92

Auchmithie (Inn)

1 mile

E. Seaton

W. Seaton

Arbroath

N
W E
S

ST CYRUS TO ARBROATH

Montrose seems almost cut off from the sea if you're travelling north – if the tide's in that is. At low tide Montrose Basin behind the town becomes a sea of mud; for naturalists it's still attractive however because there are ducks and waders in huge quantities.

Montrose itself is a fairly quiet place: there's a fine, wide high street and a museum which has been around since 1842. There's a curious collection inside, including a message in a bottle: 'No water on board, all provisions gone. Ate the dog yesterday . . .'

The tourist office in Montrose is in Bridge Street – there's also a bike shop and all the usual B&Bs, hotels, shops etc. Just south of Montrose is Lunan Bay, a beautiful sandy beach in contrast to Montrose Basin. There aren't any facilities there, so you'd have to bring your own picnic. The beach is always very quiet and the ruin of Red Castle stands gaunt above the bay.

Arbroath is a rugged red-sandstone town with a working harbour. It's famous for three things: the Declaration of Arbroath, smokies and its abbey. The Declaration of Arbroath (1320) was the declaration of Scotland's freedom from English overlordship:

FOR SO LONG AS ONE HUNDRED REMAIN ALIVE, WE WILL NEVER IN ANY DEGREE BE SUBJECT TO THE DOMINATION OF THE ENGLISH. SINCE NOT FOR GLORY, RICHES OR HONOURS DO WE FIGHT, BUT SOLELY AND ALONE FOR FREEDOM, WHICH NO GOOD MAN LOSES BUT WITH HIS LIFE.

It's worth bearing in mind that this declaration had nothing to do with democracy.

Around the harbour you'll see lots of signs advertising Arbroath smokies and you might as well try this smoked haddock while you are there. The Signal Tower Museum gives an explanation of how smokies are produced as well as information about the fishing industry.

The abbey, like most Scottish abbeys, is a splendid ruin. The above declaration was probably drafted by the abbot of the time in an effort to get international recognition of Scotland's independence. The fifteenth-century abbot's house is complete enough to give an idea of what life was like then.

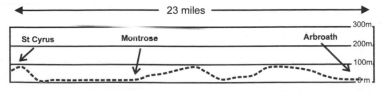

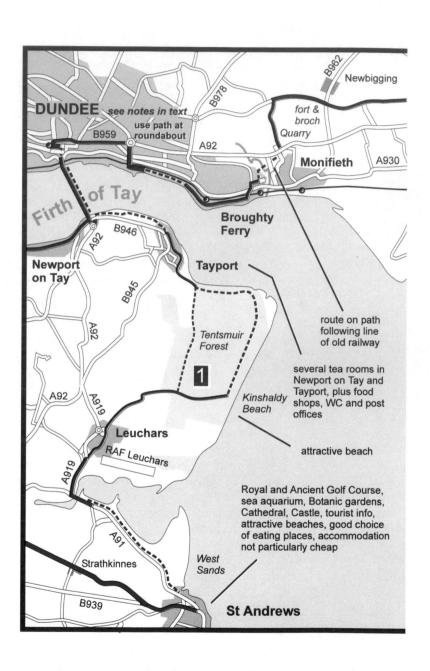

Newbigging

DUNDEE *see notes in text*
use path at
B959 *roundabout*

B978
B962

A92

fort &
broch
Quarry

Monifieth

A930

Firth of Tay

Broughty
Ferry

B946

A92

Newport
on Tay

B945

Tayport

A92

route on path
following line
of old railway

Tentsmuir
Forest

several tea rooms in
Newport on Tay and
Tayport, plus food
shops, WC and post
offices

A92

1

Kinshaldy
Beach

A919

Leuchars

attractive beach

RAF Leuchars

A919

Royal and Ancient Golf Course,
sea aquarium, Botanic gardens,
Cathedral, Castle, tourist info,
attractive beaches, good choice
of eating places, accommodation
not particularly cheap

A91

Strathkinnes

West
Sands

B939

St Andrews

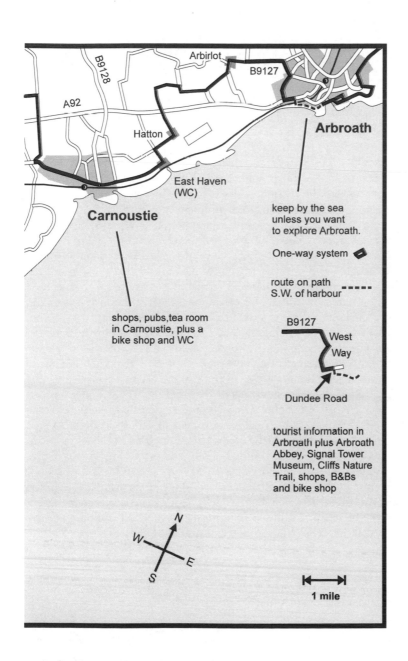

Arbirlot

B9127

B9128

A92

Hatton

Arbroath

East Haven
(WC)

Carnoustie

keep by the sea
unless you want
to explore Arbroath.

One-way system

route on path
S.W. of harbour

B9127

West
Way

Dundee Road

shops, pubs, tea room
in Carnoustie, plus a
bike shop and WC

tourist information in
Arbroath plus Arbroath
Abbey, Signal Tower
Museum, Cliffs Nature
Trail, shops, B&Bs
and bike shop

N
W   E
S

1 mile

ARBROATH TO DUNDEE

Between Arbroath and Dundee the route follows minor roads ducking either side of the A92. At Monifeith and Broughty Ferry there are sections on cyclepath.

Carnoustie has tea rooms, a bike shop and a tourist office. The train station in Golf Street is opposite the famous golf course. There's a pub, café and shops in Monifeith but by now though you are entering the conurbation of Dundee itself as Monifeith and Broughty Ferry are really suburbs.

Dundee too is famous for three things: jam, jute and journalism. The preserve made from Seville oranges called marmalade was invented in Dundee; the surrounding country produces a lot of soft fruit so jam making became a local art form. Jute of course was imported from India and made into sacks and other utilitarian things, but that's long gone. Journalism in Dundee means DC Thomson and the *Sunday Post*.

From the 1940s to the late '80s, Dundee was regarded as a city on the down – one of its daughters, the novelist A.L. Kennedy described it as 'grey grey grey'. Film makers agreed with her and filmed in the city because it seemed similar to Communist Moscow. However, these days, the city is walking blinking into the light – there is a world-class biochemistry industry through Wellcome-funded research buildings and companies, and a new multimedia arts centre. The city is trying to correct the mistakes of the 1960s by remodelling the waterfront road system and docklands. There are some severe social problems around the periphery of the city – however the opulent villas of Broughty Ferry and West Ferry show that there has been and is serious money in the city. In Broughty Ferry there are excellent pubs (e.g. the Fisherman's and Ship) as well as quality shops, yet all with a village feel to it.

The *Discovery*, the ship in which Captain Scott voyaged to the Antarctic in 1901, was built in Dundee and is now home there again. The visitor centre tells you how an expedition was organised 100 years ago and relates the story of her Captain. Quite near too is the *Unicorn*. Built in 1824 she is one of the oldest warships still in existence. Below decks beside the rows of guns there is a display about nineteenth-century naval life: ships of wood and men of iron.

Dundee also has the McManus Museum and Art Gallery. Full of

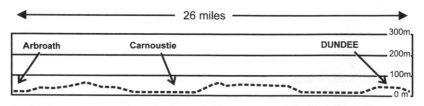

Victoriana that once graced wealthy Victorian households and sentimental paintings, it's a deft reminder of how things have changed. There's also an exhibition about Dundee's history and industry.

DUNDEE TO NEWPORT ON TAY AND ST ANDREWS

Getting to Newport is just a matter of crossing the Tay Road Bridge. Coming off the bridge go through a car park to get to the B946.

Going west from here it's a lovely quiet route along by the Firth of Tay to Newburgh. If you are travelling between Dundee and Edinburgh this is the best cycle route.

Now going east it's a lovely quiet route along by the Firth of Tay to Newport. The cycle route to St Andrews is mostly away from traffic. There are fine views of the Tay Estuary to Newport after which you pass through Tentsmuir Forest. Tentsmuir Forest unlike most forests in Scotland is flat. Kinshaldy Beach on the other side is lovely and has a remote air to it with the pines of the forest behind; it can sometimes be disturbed when a plane takes off from nearby RAF Leuchars.

St Andrews has one of the oldest universities in Britain, founded in 1411. The reflector telescope was invented here; Mary Queen of Scots planted a tree here; and the Treaty of Union between England and Scotland stipulates that it must remain open as a place of learning. The town is very well preserved and of course its golf club is recognised as the ruling body for the sport worldwide.

There are two attractive beaches, lots of interesting places to eat and some very high quality B&Bs. The Edinburgh to St Andrews Cycle Ride arrives in the town at about 5 p.m. every midsummer Saturday, and has done for the last 20 years. About 1,000 cyclists take part in this charity cycle ride for Leprosy Relief (British Leprosy Relief Association, Lepra).

Between St Andrews and Edinburgh the obvious way to go is via Kirkcaldy. There is a lot of urban cycling in this, so you might prefer to go by Falkland and Kinross as this is more rural. Thanks to the Kingdom of Fife Cycleways Project there is a choice of possible routes – see next page.

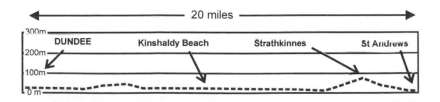

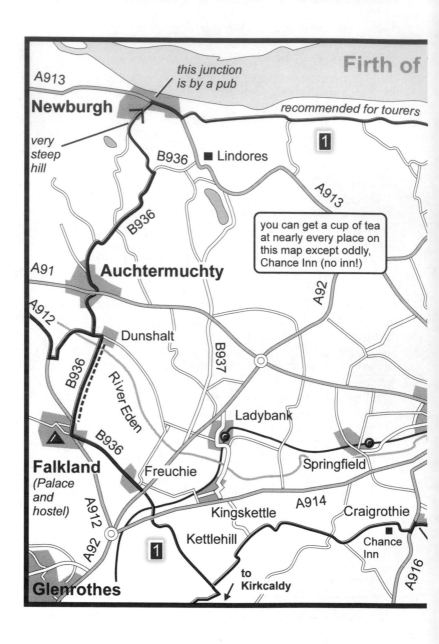

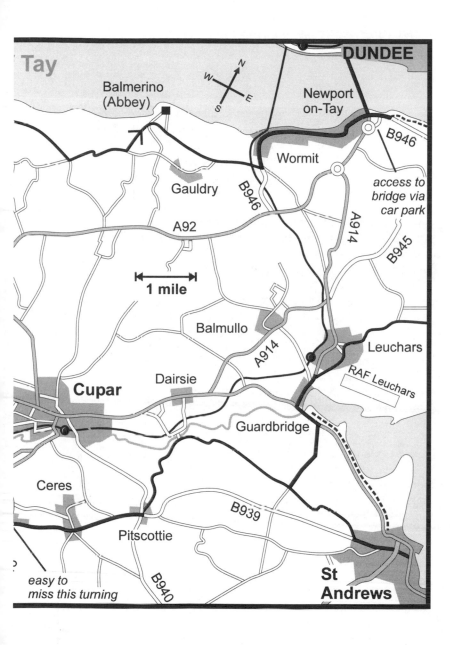

NEWPORT ON TAY TO AUCHTERMUCHTY

The map for this route is on the previous page. As mentioned earlier this is definitely the scenic way to go, it's also very quiet but quite hilly, occasionally extremely so.

Newport on Tay runs into Wormit where the railway bridge comes over from Dundee (no station). West of this the route leaves the B946 and takes to minor roads. There's a pub in Gauldry, but the route misses this out to take in an extra hill and go via Balmerino which has an abbey. This is Cistercian and dates from 1226 but is a ruin like all the others.

West of Gauldry the road climbs and dips, then just after a crossroads there's a great scenic descent to the sea overlooking the Tay Estuary. This only applies if you are going west, otherwise it's a climb with the view behind you. There are more hills before Newburgh so you'll have some descent whichever way you go. Near Newburgh there's an unusual road sign telling you to beware of crossing geese.

Newburgh was the first town in Scotland to provide free school books for pupils. It's got an attractive park overlooking Mugdrum Island. The pub opposite the park is the spot where the route turns away from the sea. There's a choice of food shops and several pubs, one with tables outside if it's sunny. It's a good place to have a rest and a bite to eat if you are continuing to Auchtermuchty as there is a serious climb.

The climb between Newburgh and Auchtermuchty goes over the shoulder of Pitcairlie Hill. Climbing up from Newburgh it's painfully steep but walking it wouldn't take too long. There's a B&B halfway up the hill at Ninewells Farm.

Auchtermuchty is the centre of the Howe of Fife farming area but its chief interest to visitors is its name which has a satisfying double 'ch' in it. The locals don't bother with this and just call it 'Muchty. There's a pub there called the Cycle Tavern but the present owner has no particular connection with bicycles so far as I know. The town went bankrupt in 1818 and the magistrates were jailed. There are some very old thatched cottages with the reeds coming from Newburgh.

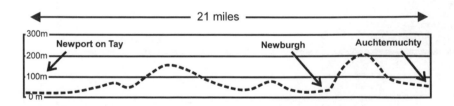

ST ANDREWS TO KETTLEHILL

The map for this route is on the previous page. This is also the route for the Edinburgh to St Andrews Cycle Ride so if you are going over it during the midsummer Saturday afternoon you'll have company.

There are pubs in Strathkinnes, Pitscottie and Craigrothie but the availability of food at these is uncertain. If you need to buy lunch much the best place is Ceres which has a good supermarket near the attractive village green, one of the few in Scotland, and a choice of other eating establishments.

When news of the victory at Bannockburn was received in Ceres, games were immediately held on the village green in celebration and they have been held annually on the village green every June since then. The Fife Folk Museum is in Ceres; housed in an interesting old building, it explains the history of rural Fife with an emphasis on ordinary people.

West of Ceres there is a very brief section on the A916; it's easy to miss the turn-off going in either direction. Despite the name, Chance Inn, a remnant of coaching days, has no inn. West of Chance Inn the route continues along a high ridge, with the farmland of the Howe of Fife far below. On a clear day you can see as far as the Grampians and the Angus Glens. You have to give way at a crossroads a mile west of Chance Inn. This needs care as you approach it quickly from either direction and visibility is poor due to trees.

The junction in Mildeans Wood by Kettlehill is a decision point, and going west takes you to Falkland. Falkland is a village really; there's an independent hostel (used to be SYHA) and some interesting pubs and tea rooms, and of course Falkland Palace. Beyond that, as far as Dunfermline, the route continues to be mainly rural if occasionally hilly.

Going south takes you to Glenrothes which is Scotland's second new town, then after that through Kirkcaldy and onto the Forth Road Bridge via Aberdour. Glenrothes has got some fine cyclepaths but going this way there is a higher proportion of urban cycling. There are good views from Burntisland and attractive sandy beaches at Aberdour, but overall the cycling quality is better via Kinross.

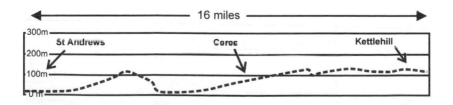

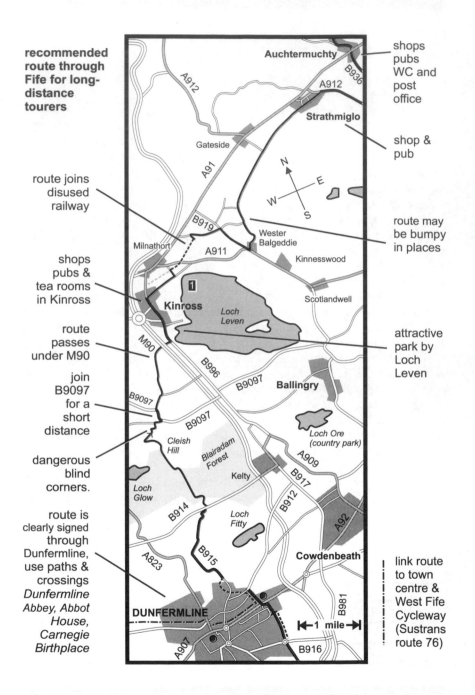

recommended route through Fife for long-distance tourers

Auchtermuchty

shops pubs WC and post office

A912

B936

A912

Strathmiglo

shop & pub

A912

Gateside

N
NE
W   E
S

A91

route joins disused railway

B919

Wester Balgeddie

route may be bumpy in places

Milnathort

A911

Kinnesswood

shops pubs & tea rooms in Kinross

1

Kinross

Loch Leven

Scotlandwell

route passes under M90

M90

attractive park by Loch Leven

join B9097 for a short distance

B996

B9097

B9097

Ballingry

B9097

Loch Ore (country park)

dangerous blind corners.

B9097

Cleish Hill

Blairadam Forest

A909

route is clearly signed through Dunfermline, use paths & crossings *Dunfermline Abbey, Abbot House, Carnegie Birthplace*

Loch Glow

Kelty

B917

B912

A92

B914

Loch Fitty

B915

Cowdenbeath

link route to town centre & West Fife Cycleway (Sustrans route 76)

A823

DUNFERMLINE

B981

A907

1 mile

B916

AUCHTERMUCHTY TO DUNFERMLINE

Falkland Palace was once a favourite hunting lodge of the Stewart kings. The palace is highly decorated with buttresses, medallions and ornate dormer windows. James V was responsible for much of the building. Famously he was not overjoyed with the news of the birth of his daughter, Mary Queen of Scots, as he wanted a male heir: 'It came wi' a lass and it'll gang wi' a lass,' he moaned.

The building is run by the National Trust for Scotland and the interiors are in the style of the seventeenth century. You can see James VI's bed and magnificent tapestries. The tennis court is the oldest in Britain and the gardens are lovely. You should be able to find a choice of places to stay as there are several hotels, B&Bs and a friendly independent hostel.

West of Falkland you pass through Strathmiglo and take to a very quiet minor road with good views of the Lomond Hills. There's a good bar-lunch pub at Wester Balgeddie just north of Loch Leven.

Kinross tourist office is unfortunately not in the town itself but right in the middle of the nearby motorway service station. There is however a choice of pubs, hotels and tea rooms and if the weather is warm you can buy food in one of the shops and picnic by Loch Leven. You can take a boat out to Loch Leven Castle on the island.

South of Kinross the route runs through rolling farmland then climbs over the Cleish Hill; to the north there are good views over Loch Leven but views to the south are obscured by the forest.

Dunfermline was a royal favourite too, the king sitting 'in Dunfermline toun, drinking the bluid-red wine'. Edward I of England burned the abbey in 1303, claiming the Scots had turned it into a den of thieves by holding their rebellious parliaments there. It is the burial place for Scottish kings, the most famous being Robert the Bruce. Dunfermline is also the birth place of Robert Carnegie, the American steel millionaire and philanthropist.

There is a network of cycle routes running through the town, a mixture of on- and off-road routes. Mostly they are aimed at improving cycle access for local people but the National Cycle Network route (also called the Kingdom Route) is signposted.

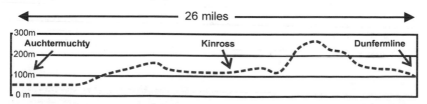

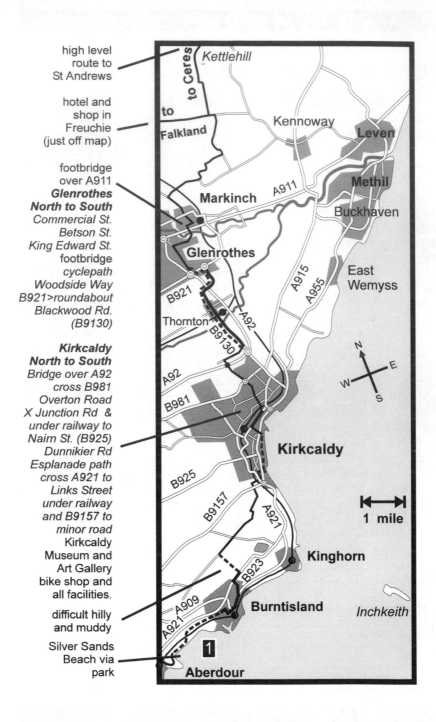

high level route to St Andrews

hotel and shop in Freuchie (just off map)

footbridge over A911
Glenrothes
North to South
Commercial St.
Betson St.
King Edward St.
footbridge
cyclepath
Woodside Way
B921>roundabout
Blackwood Rd.
(B9130)

Kirkcaldy
North to South
Bridge over A92
cross B981
Overton Road
X Junction Rd &
under railway to
Nairn St. (B925)
Dunnikier Rd
Esplanade path
cross A921 to
Links Street
under railway
and B9157 to
minor road
Kirkcaldy
Museum and
Art Gallery
bike shop and
all facilities.

difficult hilly and muddy

Silver Sands Beach via park

Kettlehill

to Ceres

to Falkland

Kennoway

Leven

Methil

Markinch

A911

Buckhaven

Glenrothes

East Wemyss

A915

A955

B921

A92

Thornton

B9130

A92

B981

N
E
W
S

B925

Kirkcaldy

B9157

A921

1 mile

Kinghorn

B923

Burntisland

Inchkeith

A909

A921

1

Aberdour

KETTLEHILL TO ABERDOUR

There is quite a lot of urban cycling in this section with the route using a mixture of rural roads, urban back streets, cycle lanes on busier roads and dedicated cyclepaths. The route is well signposted but the signs sometimes compete with a huge number of urban signs so a sharp eye is necessary.

Markinch, now a suburb of Glenrothes, is historically a paper-making and distilling town. It has a train station, shops and toilets. South of Markinch you have to cross over the A911 on a footbridge.

Glenrothes is Scotland's second new town and because of this it's got a high proportion of cyclepaths segregated from normal traffic. A map of all the routes in Glenrothes is available from the Kingdom of Fife Cycleways (see Appendix). This route though is largely separate as it skirts the town to the east. To get to the town centre from the National Route you continue west on the cyclepath at the junction of Woodside Way and Bighty Avenue instead of going north–south along Woodside Way.

Kirkcaldy is an industrial town but it has some fine parks and an attractive sea front. Its old nickname, 'the Lang Toun', derives from its long high street which is Fife's biggest shopping centre. It was the birth place of Adam Smith, author of *The Wealth of Nations*, and he is commemorated in the Adam Smith Centre. The architect Robert Adam went to the same school in Kirkcaldy as did Adam Smith; the other person associated with Kirkcaldy is Michael Nairn, inventor of linoleum.

Kinghorn and Aberdour both have sandy beaches and are popular places to visit in the summer. The route bypasses Kinghorn but Aberdour is probably the more attractive of the two with a lovely beach at Silver Sands Bay (café in summer). The route passes through it.

Burntisland was a ship building centre and more recently has got some North Sea oil contracts. It's not a particularly attractive town but the area by the beach is pleasant. There is a funfair in summer and the Edwardian Fair Museum. As you will see on the map, just north of Burntisland the route leaves the B923 and cuts north across open land. This is a very steep climb with a poor surface, possibly muddy in wet weather. When this will be improved is unclear.

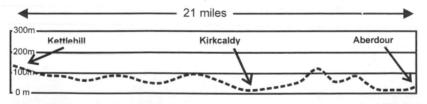

on road cycle
lanes B981

Aberdour - Inverkeithing
(bike shop) follow the coast

good bar lunches at
the Woodside Hotel

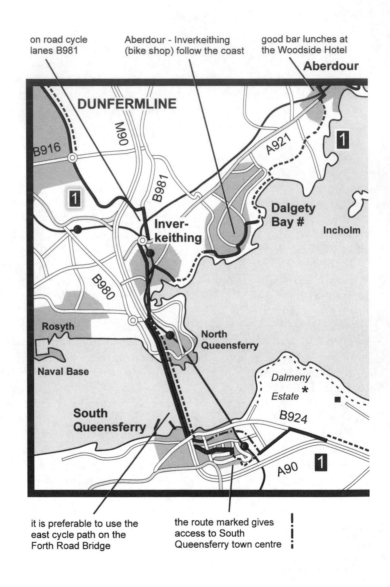

it is preferable to use the
east cycle path on the
Forth Road Bridge

the route marked gives
access to South
Queensferry town centre

\# mixture of coastal path with rural feel and housing estates at Dalgety Bay, good views

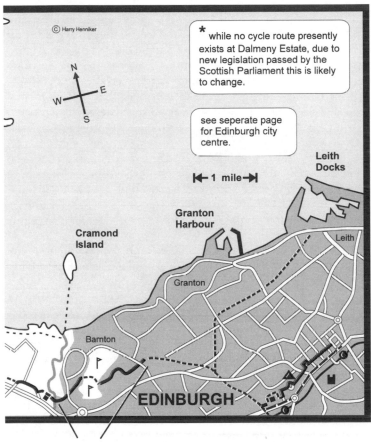

© Harry Henniker

N
W — E
S

* while no cycle route presently exists at Dalmeny Estate, due to new legislation passed by the Scottish Parliament this is likely to change.

see seperate page for Edinburgh city centre.

Leith Docks

◄— 1 mile —►

Granton Harbour

Cramond Island

Leith

Granton

Barnton

EDINBURGH

east to west Cyclepath, *Silverknowes Drive > Terrace, X Crammond Rd. S. to Barnton Avenue, path between golf courses, Barnton Ave W. X Whitehouse Road to Braepark Road, cross River Almond.*

ABERDOUR AND DUNFERMLINE TO EDINBURGH

This journey is a daily trial to commuters who live in Fife and work in Edinburgh, but they mostly drive there or get the train. The experience on a bike is rather different.

North of the Firth of Forth the route between Aberdour and Inverkeithing mostly follows the coast, ducking inland only to avoid the oil terminal opposite Inchcolm Island. Dalgety Bay is mostly housing estates; the route skirts round by the sea as far as possible. To get through Inverkeithing it takes to minor roads then on-road cycle lanes on the B981.

Coming from Dunfermline the route crosses over the M90 motorway then joins the B981. You could divert to North Queensferry to visit Deep Sea World, probably the nearest experience you can get to actually being under the sea without getting wet.

Crossing the Forth on the Forth Road Bridge is worth taking your time over. The spectacular Forth Rail Bridge, or simply the Forth Bridge, one of the greatest engineering feats in the world, was built between 1883 and 1890. The bridge cost £3,177,206. One of the engineers when asked how long it would last, replied, 'Forever if you look after it.' Looking after it is mostly a matter of painting.

If you aren't in a hurry it's worth dropping down to South Queensferry; paths from the south end of the road bridge lead underneath it giving access to the town. This is a worthwhile day trip from Edinburgh.

Between South Queensferry and Edinburgh the route is virtually all traffic-free apart from a short stretch on the B924 near South Queensferry. You pass over the old Cramond Brig, just east of the dual carriageway. From here a cycle route runs downstream to the old village of Cramond with its yachts and an interesting restaurant by the river. There are not a few steps to negotiate though!

The major cycling routes through Edinburgh are given here but if you would like more detailed information Spokes, The Lothian Cycle Campaign, produces a city cycling map. You can get this from most city bike shops and bookshops or directly from Spokes (see Appendix).

Donaldson's College, a school for the deaf, is a turreted building in

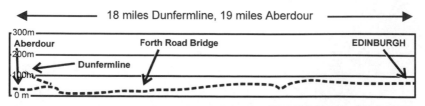

18 miles Dunfermline, 19 miles Aberdour

300m
Aberdour — Forth Road Bridge — EDINBURGH
200m
Dunfermline
100m
0 m

playing fields. At the time of writing the cycle route round the back of it was not open.

There are on-road cycle lanes on West Coates. The cyclepath on the other side of West Coates is now open.

Between Donaldson's College and Queensferry Street the route follows fairly quiet streets in the New Town. At the end of Melville Street cross over into what seems a cul-de-sac; a little lane takes you up the side of the dome of West Register House and you are in Charlotte Square.

The best you can say about George Street for cycling is that the parallel Queen Street is worse. Princes Street has cycle / bus lanes, though it could be improved in the coming years when cars may be banned entirely. The long dash line by the side of Lothian Road is a path carried over the West Approach Road on a fancy high-tech bridge (access from Rutland Square).

There are maps on other pages showing the routes south and west from Edinburgh; taken together they show the best ways in and out of the city. If you want to spend more time cycling in Edinburgh buy the cycle map produced by Spokes.

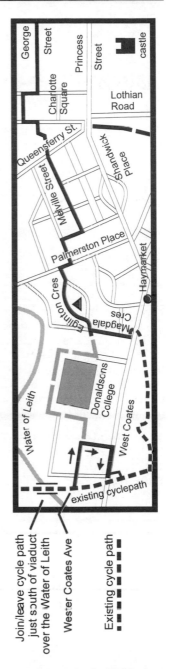

8

EDINBURGH–BERWICK ON TWEED

TOTAL DISTANCE – 87 MILES
FOR EDINBURGH TO BERWICK START AT PAGE 157
FOR BERWICK TO EDINBURGH START AT PAGE 169
  AND WORK BACKWARDS

INTRODUCTION

The northern part of this route is in central Scotland but most of it, south of Temple, is in the Borders. Once the scene of fierce conflict, the Borders still has a culture that is distinctively its own. This is most apparent during the annual Common Riding, where the Borderers ride on horseback to preserve their boundaries. The one held at Selkirk dates from the Battle of Flodden in 1513. This is not a spectacle for tourists, but an annual event in which the whole community takes part.

This route is mainly on minor roads, which offer quiet rides in lovely scenery. There are plenty of things to look at, including abbeys and great houses, and no lack of cosy pubs and tea rooms. The gradients are reasonably gentle in the river valleys, but crossing between them will involve a climb. East of Kelso the route becomes easier, through gently rolling farmland to Berwick on Tweed.

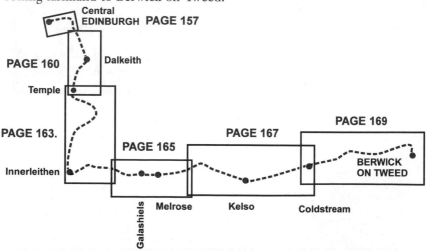

CENTRAL EDINBURGH TO INNOCENT RAILWAY LINE

The map for this section is on the next page. Some of the other routes in this book also terminate in Edinburgh – you might find the notes on other pages helpful.

Going south the route takes you across Princes Street, using a cyclists-only right turn, then by the side of the Greek temple called the Royal Scottish Academy. After this it climbs the Mound, the side of the road being marked as a cycle lane, and crosses the Royal Mile (High Street) at traffic lights. The next major junction is by the new sandstone rotunda of the National Museum of Scotland. There are cycle lanes here, but if you have children it's best to walk.

Get off your bike at the museum, walk 15 metres in the same direction, and cross the road to the wide pavement on Forrest Road. The statue of a dog, Greyfriars Bobby, will be on the same side. You can identify that by the tourists surrounding it taking photographs. Walk south away from Bobby and cross on to the Meadows cyclepath using the light-controlled crossing.

Ride down the hill and at the bottom turn left to another cyclepath. Turn left into Buccleuch Street at a police box (now a coffee stall), then immediately right into Gifford Park. After that refer to the map. The Engine Shed Café is a good tea stop, incidentally.

The first part of the Innocent cycle path can be quite cool going south, as you whizz down the tunnel. You're only going to be in it for about 90 seconds however and hopefully you'll emerge into warm sunshine.

A plaque can be seen here giving the history of the Innocent railway, which was opened in 1831 to carry coal to the city. Riding on the horse-drawn trains became popular and the railway company rapidly converted wagons to coaches to carry passengers. The line was converted to a cyclepath in 1985 after a long campaign by local cyclists (Spokes).

Take care crossing Duddingston Road then continue along the cyclepath again. When you get to a second road crossing, where a burn (possibly with shopping trolleys in it) runs beside the path, you're at Niddrie – see next section.

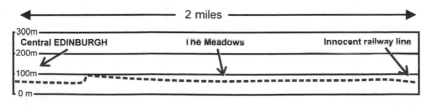

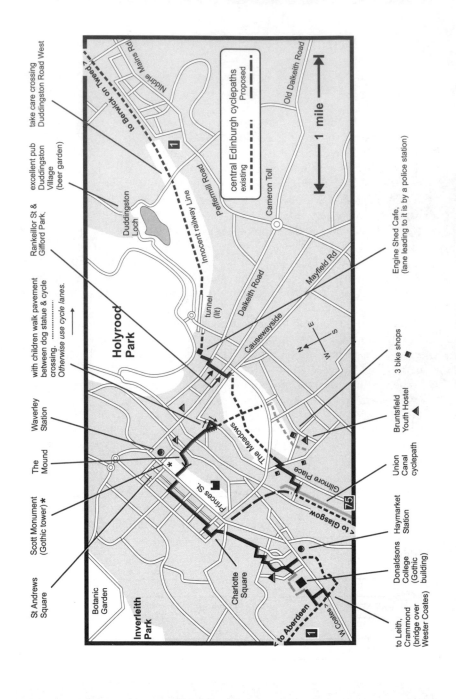

St Andrews Square

Scott Monument (Gothic tower) *

The Mound

Waverley Station

with children walk pavement between dog statue & cycle crossing. ....
Otherwise use cycle lanes.

Rankeillor St & Gifford Park.

excellent pub Duddingston Village (beer garden)

take care crossing Duddingston Road West

Botanic Garden

Inverleith Park

Holyrood Park

Duddingston Loch

Niddrie Mains Rd

to Berwick on Tweed >

Innocent railway Line

Peffermill Road

Old Dalkeith Road

Cameron Toll

1 mile

central Edinburgh cyclepaths
existing
Proposed

tunnel (lit)

Dalkeith Road

Mayfield Rd

Causewayside

Princes St.

The Meadows

N
E
S
W

Charlotte Square

Gilmore Place

75

< to Glasgow

Engine Shed Cafe, (lane leading to it is by a police station)

3 bike shops

Bruntsfield Youth Hostel

Union Canal cyclepath

Haymarket Station

Donaldsons College (Gothic building)

W Coates

1

< to Aberdeen

to Leith, Crammond (bridge over Wester Coates)

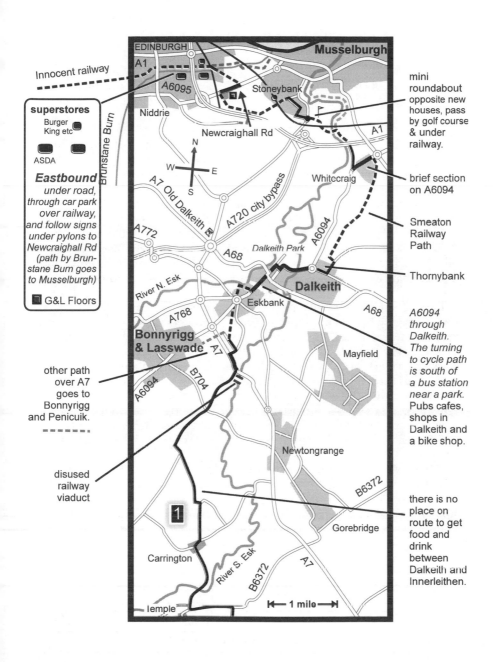

Innocent railway

superstores

Burger King etc

ASDA

Eastbound
under road,
through car park
over railway,
and follow signs
under pylons to
Newcraighall Rd
(path by Brun-
stane Burn goes
to Musselburgh)

G&L Floors

other path
over A7
goes to
Bonnyrigg
and Penicuik.

disused
railway
viaduct

EDINBURGH

A1

A6095

Niddrie

Brunstane Burn

Newcraighall Rd

Stoneybank

Musselburgh

A1

N
W   E
S

A7 Old Dalkeith Rd

A720 city bypass

Whitecraig

A6094

A772

A68

Dalkeith Park

Dalkeith

A68

River N. Esk

Eskbank

A768

Bonnyrigg
& Lasswade

A7

A6094

B704

Mayfield

Newtongrange

B6372

1

Gorebridge

Carrington

River S. Esk

B6372

A7

Temple

⊢— 1 mile —⊣

mini
roundabout
opposite new
houses, pass
by golf course
& under
railway.

brief section
on A6094

Smeaton
Railway
Path

Thornybank

A6094
through
Dalkeith.
The turning
to cycle path
is south of
a bus station
near a park.
Pubs cafes,
shops in
Dalkeith and
a bike shop.

there is no
place on
route to get
food and
drink
between
Dalkeith and
Innerleithen.

INNOCENT RAILWAY LINE TO DALKEITH

The map for this is on the previous page. The route should be clearly signed but I'm including directions in the text with lots of street names so that if you go astray you can ask. The instructions assume you are leaving Edinburgh.

At the east end of the Innocent railway line you cross another road (Duddingston Park South); a dirt cyclepath continues in the same direction following Brunstane Burn. Continue straight on ignoring the superstores etc. and pass under a road to a car park, cross this and the railway on a footbridge.

A cyclepath continues by the burn, don't take this (it goes to Musselburgh) but cross over the burn on an old bridge. This is signposted and leads you past a housing estate (Gilbertstoun) and the old Brunstane House to Newcraighall Road. If any signs are missing note that the route follows underneath a line of electricity pylons here. You emerge on Newcraighall Road on a cyclepath. *Coming in the other direction look for concrete bollards.*

Turn right, or west, for 400 metres, cycling along Newcraighall Road and passing under a railway line, then turn left to another cyclepath. This takes you near the city bypass a little way and ends near Musselburgh train station. Another right turn takes you through a housing estate (Stoneybank / Mucklets), you cross Old Craighall Road at a mini-roundabout to Ferguson Drive. This becomes a dirt path going under a railway and past Monktonhall Golf Course then you go over the River Esk on a metal footbridge. Turn right to go upstream; when you meet a road bear right to continue in the same direction still following the river. Turn left on to the A6094 to enter Whitecraig; at the far side turn right to another cyclepath. This takes you to Dalkeith.

While other small towns near Edinburgh may be little more than dormitory suburbs Dalkeith has always been its own place. It's the county town for Midlothian and still has agricultural connections. There's a bike shop and Dalkeith Estate, which has facilities for children and attractive walks, is worth visiting. If you need to buy food get it here as the route now leads away from shops to open country.

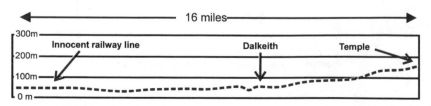

DALKEITH TO TEMPLE

The map for this is on the previous page. Beyond Eskbank the route uses a minor road to get to Carrington and Temple and route-finding is easy after then. Some care is necessary to find the route through Eskbank. The description assumes you are leaving Edinburgh.

You leave Dalkeith passing a bus station then a park, the cyclepath is a right turn just after this. Unfortunately this section is likely to disappear when the railway to the borders is re-opened.

Going in the other direction, after passing the former Eskbank Station on the cyclepath you go under Lasswade Road then turn right at a cyclepath junction. Going in either direction if you find yourself on the River Esk Viaduct you've missed a turning.

The route then leads you to the A7, note that a cycle / footbridge over the A7 near here is not the way to go (that leads to Lasswade). There is a brief section on the A7 (take care) then you turn right under the arch of an old railway viaduct and you're in the countryside.

The road now runs through rolling farmland. The Pentland Hills can be seen to the west and ahead lie the Moorfoot Hills which you will be passing through. Over to the east are Gorebridge and Mayfield.

Carrington is an attractive old village – sandstone cottages with red pantiled roofs. The church is slightly unusual as it has been converted into a doo'cot.

Temple is on a steep bank of the River Esk and is noteable for its thirteenth century church. It was a former seat of the Knights Templar from which the name derives. In the churchyard is the gravestone of the Rev. James Goldie. Rev. Goldie clearly believed in taking no chances as his will is engraved on his gravestone. Whether he had this done before his death or not is unclear.

You may notice that the road between Temple and Carrington follows the bank of the River Esk some of the time. Not that long ago it slid into the river, so isolating Temple from Carrington. The local council felt that it would be too expensive to repair so proposed to close the road. This caused much anger in Temple and Carrington as they share a village hall, and the council eventually relented.

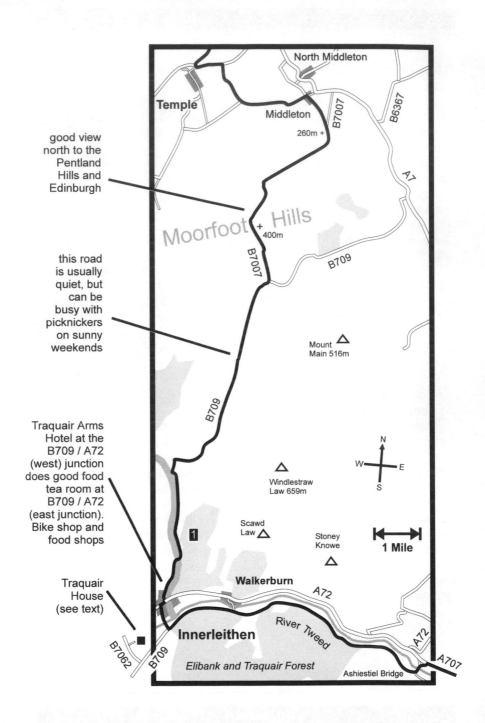

North Middleton

Temple

Middleton

B7007

B6367

260m +

A7

good view
north to the
Pentland
Hills and
Edinburgh

Moorfoot Hills

+
400m

B7007

B709

this road
is usually
quiet, but
can be
busy with
picknickers
on sunny
weekends

Mount
Main 516m △

B709

N
W E
S

Traquair Arms
Hotel at the
B709 / A72
(west) junction
does good food
tea room at
B709 / A72
(east junction).
Bike shop and
food shops

Windlestraw
Law 659m △

Scawd
Law △

Stoney
Knowe △

|◀━━▶|
1 Mile

1

Walkerburn

A72

Traquair
House
(see text)

Traquair
House
(see text)

River Tweed

B7062

B709

Innerleithen

A72

A72

A707

Elibank and Traquair Forest

Ashiestiel Bridge

TEMPLE TO ASHIESTIEL BRIDGE

South of Temple the countryside seems surprisingly remote considering how close you are to Edinburgh. There's a steady climb or a fast descent as you cross the Moorfoot escarpment, then a series of up and downs before the road descends towards Innerleithen. Just north of Innerleithen you run by a golf course before entering the town.

Innerleithen lies at the junction of the Rivers Tweed and Leithen. It's a pleasant little town with an excellent bike shop which caters for mountain bikers cycling in the nearby Elibank and Traquair Forest. It has a mineral spring, made famous by Sir Walter Scott's novel *St Ronan's Well*, which is now named after the book.

The first woollen mill was built by a Traquair blacksmith who had made a fortune in London. This is still in existence (Caerles Mill). Border Games are held annually and include a pageant of St Ronan ridding the town of the devil for the next 12 months.

Quite near Innerleithen (see map) is Traquair House, claimed to be the oldest inhabited house in Scotland. This is probably correct as it dates from the tenth century. Though it's very much lived in, it's open to the public and is worth a short diversion. Twenty-seven kings and queens have stayed there, and you can see examples of Mary Queen of Scots' embroidery and innumerable other historical treasures. The house and the gardens are delightful and the interior is furnished with original decorations and furniture. There's also an excellent tea room.

After Innerleithen the route follows the south bank of the River Tweed downstream. No river has perhaps been responsible for so much romantic literature as the Tweed – James Hogg the Ettrick Shepherd, Sir Walter Scott and the anonymous composers of the Border ballads all wrote about it. You might assume that 'tweed', the cloth, is called after the river but oddly that is not so. In fact it comes from a misreading in London of the technical word 'tweel'.

Anyway, the River Tweed is as lovely as it ever was between Innerleithen and Ashiestiel Bridge, and on the way it passes Walkerburn, another small mill town. There is a food shop, the Scottish Museum of Wool Textiles and you can get a cup of tea in Walkerburn.

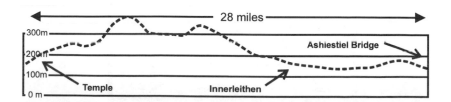

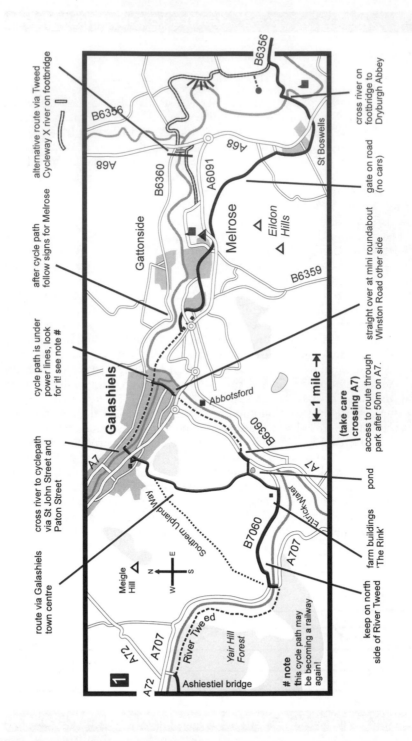

1

A72

A707

A72

River Tweed

Ashiestiel bridge

Yair Hill Forest

Meigle Hill

Southern Upland Way

note
this cycle path may be becoming a railway again!

keep on north side of River Tweed

B7060

A707

farm buildings 'The Rink'

Ettrick Water

pond

Galashiels

A7

Abbotsford

B6360

access to route through park after 50m on A7.

(take care crossing A7)

← 1 mile →

straight over at mini roundabout Winston Road other side

B6359

Melrose

Eildon Hills

A6091

B6360

Gattonside

A68

St Boswells

gate on road (no cars)

cross river on footbridge to Dryburgh Abbey

B6356

B6356

A68

alternative route via Tweed Cycleway X river on footbridge

after cycle path follow signs for Melrose

cycle path is under power lines, look for it! see note #

cross river to cyclepath via St John Street and Paton Street

route via Galashiels town centre

N
E
W
S

ASHIESTIEL BRIDGE TO DRYBURGH ABBEY

Ashiestiel Bridge is a lovely old bridge in a beautiful spot so it's worth lingering. Currently east of that you used to cycle on the A707 for a mile or two. Now you can avoid this by remaining on the south side of the river, going by Yair (see map). The National Cycle Route here partly duplicates the Tweed Cycleway, though the two routes are not exactly the same. I've shown where they differ on the map. Use either, or maybe use parts of each, to make a circular day ride.

The Galashiels / Melrose area is the most populated area of the borders, but it's still mostly pretty. The route uses a cyclepath in Galashiels to avoid the busiest area of the town and that's the way to go. Sustrans also offers you an option via Galashiels town centre (see map). To my mind it's much simpler and easier to cycle through the park by the River Tweed. You could always nip up the cyclepath to the town, where there is a bike shop.

Galashiels is first and foremost a wool town. Wool mills were in existence here from 1622 but the main development came in the nineteenth century. The Scottish College of Textiles is here; nowadays there's other light industry stretching towards Melrose. Abbotsford, Sir Walter Scott's house is quite near, on the other side of the River Tweed. You'll see it on the far bank as you cycle down. It's open to the public from March to October, and is full of curiosities relating to his novels.

Melrose Abbey was founded in 1136 and was finally destroyed by the Earl of Hertford in 1544. The remains are impressive; look for a figure of a pig playing the bagpipes. The former railway station has been restored and now contains a tea room and craft shop, though it would be better if it was still a railway station. Other options are the Abbey Coffee Shop, or Marmion's Brasserie. The excellent youth hostel is behind the abbey. Melrose is prettier than Galashiels, and there are some attractive walks by the river. The hills behind the town are the Eildons. You get a good view of them from the cyclepath and an even better view from Scott's View (viewpoint on map). The Tweed Cycleway takes in Scott's View and the elegant Leaderfoot Viaduct; the National Route does not.

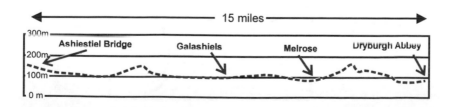

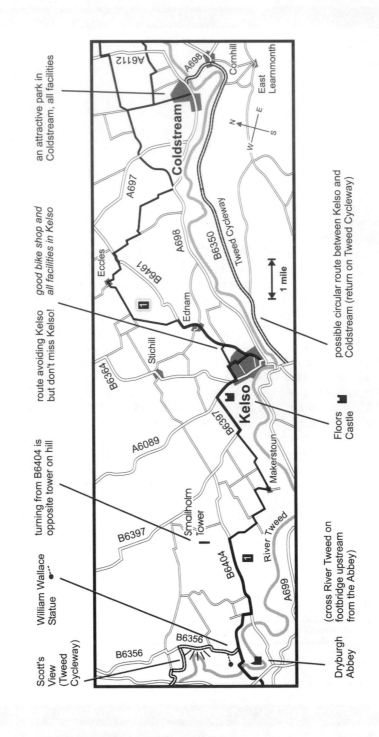

an attractive park in
Coldstream, all facilities

good bike shop and
all facilities in Kelso

route avoiding Kelso
but don't miss Kelso!

turning from B6404 is
opposite tower on hill

Scott's View
(Tweed Cycleway)

William Wallace
Statue

possible circular route between Kelso and
Coldstream (return on Tweed Cycleway)

Floors
Castle

(cross River Tweed on
footbridge upstream
from the Abbey)

Dryburgh
Abbey

Coldstream

Kelso

A6112

A698

Cornhill

East
Learnmonth

N
E
W
S

A697

A698

Tweed Cycleway

B6350

Eccles

B6461

Ednam

Stichill

B6364

1

1 mile

B6397

A6089

Makerstoun

Smailholm
Tower

B6397

B6404

1

River Tweed

A699

B6356

B6356

DRYBURGH ABBEY TO COLDSTREAM

What the National Cycle Route does take in, but the Tweed Cycleway doesn't, is Dryburgh Abbey. Before getting there it passes round Newtown St Boswells. This is pleasantly spread out and has shops and hotels.

Dryburgh Abbey has a beautiful setting in a horseshoe bend of the Tweed; despite being destroyed by the English three times, the cloister buildings have survived fairly completely. The cycle route crosses over to the abbey on a footbridge over the River Tweed. There is a statue of William Wallace up a track just north of the abbey (see map).

Between Dryburgh Abbey and Kelso the route meanders along, mostly on minor roads north of the river. As you approach Kelso the countryside becomes gentler. The route has an option of bypassing Kelso but doing this would be a shame.

Kelso is worth lingering in. Follow the signs for the town centre and the Tweed Cycleway. The cobbled town square is particularly elegant. Sir Walter Scott thought it was the most beautiful town in Scotland – apart from being infested with cars the town centre has hardly changed. The abbey is near the town square; you'll pass the bike shop on the way to it.

The bridge over the River Tweed at Kelso was the model for Waterloo Bridge on the Thames, being designed by the same engineer, John Rennie. Floors Castle is just to the north. Originally designed by William Adam, it's an enormous place, so you should allow plenty of time. You don't need to pay to get into the excellent tea room.

Between Kelso and Coldstream the Sustrans route and the Tweed Cycleway go different ways. The Sustrans route is the better choice but using both to make a circular route would be an attractive day trip.

Coldstream like Gretna is right next to the Scottish border, and like Gretna has an 'Old Marriage House' for similar reasons. Coldstream is attractive too, maybe not so elegant as Kelso but the park by the river is a good place to picnic. The Coldstream Guards were established here and eventually became the 'King's Men'. Quite near too is The Hirsel, former home of Sir Alec Douglas Home, and a bird sanctuary.

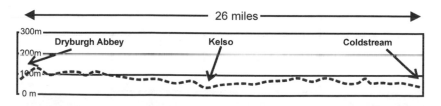

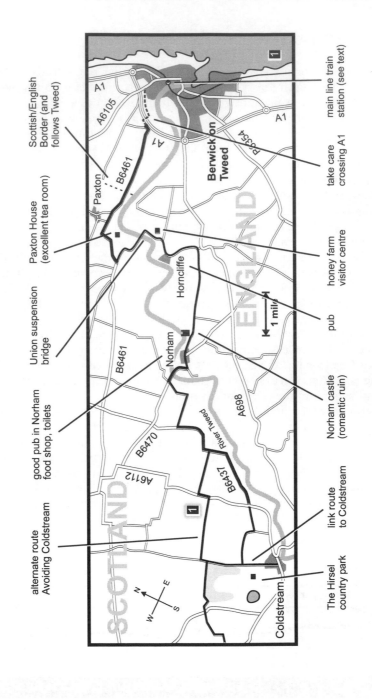

main line train
station (see text)

Scottish/English
Border (and
follows Tweed)

take care
crossing A1

Paxton House
(excellent tea room)

honey farm
visitor centre

Union suspension
bridge

pub

good pub in Norham
food shop, toilets

Norham castle
(romantic ruin)

alternate route
Avoiding Coldstream

link route
to Coldstream

The Hirsel
country park

A1

A6105

B6461

Paxton

Berwick on
Tweed

B6354

A1

ENGLAND

Horncliffe

1 mile

Norham

B6461

A698

River Tweed

B6470

A6112

B6437

1

SCOTLAND

N
E
S
W

Coldstream

COLDSTREAM TO BERWICK ON TWEED

The River Tweed is the border now between England and Scotland. This used to be the case all the way to the sea but Scotland didn't manage to hang on to Berwick, and it was finally surrendered to England in 1482. This made for the rather odd situation of Berwick not being in Berwickshire.

The route rolls along through fairly flat country eventually crossing the Tweed near Norham. There's a castle just outside Norham and a pub doing bar lunches in the centre. The route crosses over into Scotland again on the romantic Union Suspension Bridge, the first suspension bridge of any size in Britain. Before that you pass a honey farm. This has a visitor centre where you can see the bees in action and also buy honey. The life cycle of the bees is throughly explained.

Shortly after this there's Paxton House, one of the best Adam mansions in the country, and there's a romantic story attached to it. On 23 August 1750 the heir to Paxton Estate, Patrick Home, pledged his love to Sophie de Brandt in Berlin. He returned to build a house for her and commissioned the Adam brothers to build a mansion of pink sandstone. She never came, as King Frederick of Prussia made it impossible. Sophie never married.

Finally going east you cross the border for the last time and roll towards Berwick on Tweed. Before you get there you have to cross the A1. A traffic island in the middle makes it easier but cars still race by at over 70mph so allow plenty of time. Between the A1 and Berwick there's a short section of cyclepath, then you're on roads. You pass the train station as you enter the town.

Berwick has a museum in the old barracks and impressive ramparts. These didn't prevent the town changing hands between the Scots and the English 13 times until it was finally surrendered to England. There are lots of facilities here including a bike shop. The main railway line between Edinburgh and London passes through here. Not all trains stop but many do. Space for bikes is limited; book your bike in advance. Sustrans Route 1 continues south from Berwick but that is beyond the scope of this present book as it's all England.

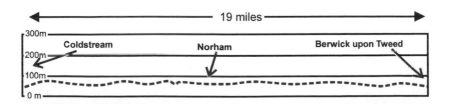

9

DUNDEE–PITLOCHRY

TOTAL DISTANCE 55 MILES
FOR DUNDEE TO PITLOCHRY START AT PAGE 172
FOR PITLOCHRY TO DUNDEE SEE PAGE 177
   AND WORK BACKWARDS

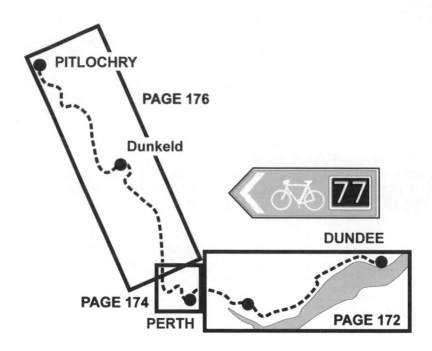

INTRODUCTION

This route was recently introduced and this is the first full description of it. Mostly it's on quiet rural roads though there are some cyclepath sections in Dundee, Perth and Dunkeld. It connects to Route 1 (Aberdeen to Edinburgh) at Dundee and Route 7 (Glasgow to Inverness) near Pitlochry.

In Dundee the cycle path also forms part of the Dundee Green Circular, a 26-mile bike ride going round the edge of the city. West of this it runs through the Carse of Gowrie on the north side of the Firth of Tay then it cuts north over the Braes of Carse to Perth.

Perth was once the capital of Scotland but this moved to Edinburgh in 1437 after the murder of James I in Perth. The route through Perth is mostly in parkland, following the River Tay and then the River Almond. If you want to explore the city of Perth you'll have to leave the route.

After Perth the route goes through beautiful wooded countryside amidst rolling hills to Dunkeld. This is a historic little town on the banks of the River Tay with a cathedral, partly ruined, dating back to the thirteenth century. There are many restored old houses from the seventeenth century. After Dunkeld the route winds north again, following the River Tay, then crossing it on a former railway bridge. After this you follow the River Tummel, finally ending at Pitlochry.

Pitlochry seems at first glance to be a seaside resort marooned in the middle of the Highlands, but look more closely – it has plenty of charms. Perthshire is one of the most beautiful areas of Scotland. It combines Highland scenery with many lochs and rivers. There's something particularly great about rolling along on your bike next to water. There are plenty of other opportunities to do this near Pitlochry. Route 7 (Lochs and Glens North) connects to this one just south of Pitlochry (at Logierait) and follows the River Tay to Loch Tay.

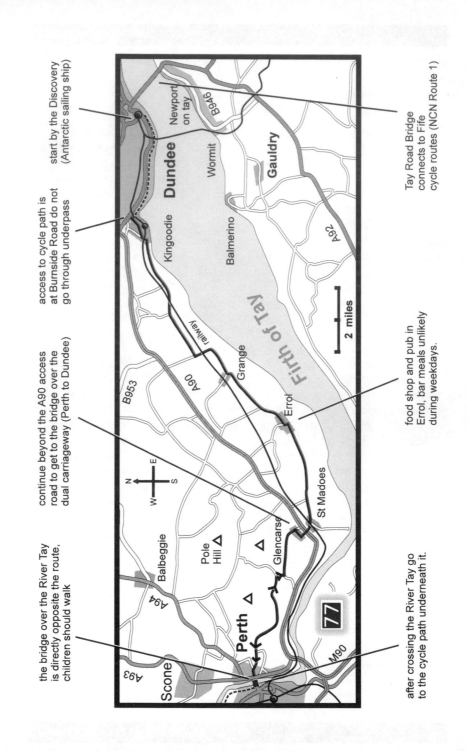

the bridge over the River Tay is directly opposite the route, children should walk

continue beyond the A90 access road to get to the bridge over the dual carriageway (Perth to Dundee)

access to cycle path is at Burnside Road do not go through underpass

start by the Discovery (Antarctic sailing ship)

Tay Road Bridge connects to Fife cycle routes (NCN Route 1)

food shop and pub in Errol, bar meals unlikely during weekdays.

after crossing the River Tay go to the cycle path underneath it.

Scone

A93

Balbeggie

A94

Perth

Pole Hill △

△

Glencarse

St Madoes

M90

77

B953

A90

railway

Grange

Errol

Firth of Tay

Kingoodie

Dundee

Newport on tay

B946

Wormit

Balmerino

Gauldry

A92

N
E
S
W

2 miles

DUNDEE TO PERTH

Start by the *Discovery*, the ship used by Captain Scott to explore Antartica. This is opposite Dundee train station and by the Tay Road Bridge (Kingdom of Fife Cycle Routes). Follow the promenade west following Route 77 signs. You can see the piers of the old railway bridge. It collapsed into the sea on 28 December 1879 taking 75 souls with it. Perhaps appropriately you cycle over a piece of doggerel about it by William McGonagall, Scotland's worst poet. After a short distance the promenade ends at a fast food cabin; the cyclepath leaves the shore to run by the A85.

Take care crossing the various slip roads leading to the airport, the council tip etc. After three miles the route leaves the Dundee Circular cycle route (which goes through an underpass). Avoid the underpass, keep straight on to Burnside Road (opposite direction look for this). In Invergowrie turn left to pass Invergowrie Station. You meet the coast again at Kingoodie.

Kingoodie owes its origin to nearby quarries which supplied building stone for several centuries. The stone was used for for harbour works and sea walls. The coast here has been designated as a nature reserve, it supports a great variety of bird life on the tidal mudflats.

There's a slight climb to Errol which gives views of the area, the Carse of Gowrie. This traditionally was a fruit-growing area, giving rise to a jam-making industry in Dundee. In Errol food may be available at the Old Smiddy Inn. There's also a food shop. You can reliably get food at the Village Inn in Glencarse.

Soon the easy hills are at an end however, as you cross above the busy A90 dual carriageway to Glencarse (in the opposite direction don't go on to the A90). Continuing to Perth there's a very steep hill but there are great views once you get to the top. There are a number of woodland walks (some can be ridden) in Kinnoul Hill Woodland Park which you pass. This includes the famous one to the cliff-top viewpoint with the folly. Naturally there's a descent to Perth. Take care at the descent to the traffic lights which lead directly across to the bridge over the River Tay.

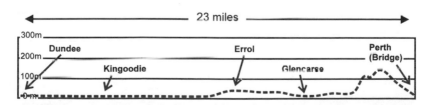

should be pubs serving
food in Almondbank and
Pitcairngreen

it is possible to go on the gravel path
but this is not the official route (yet)

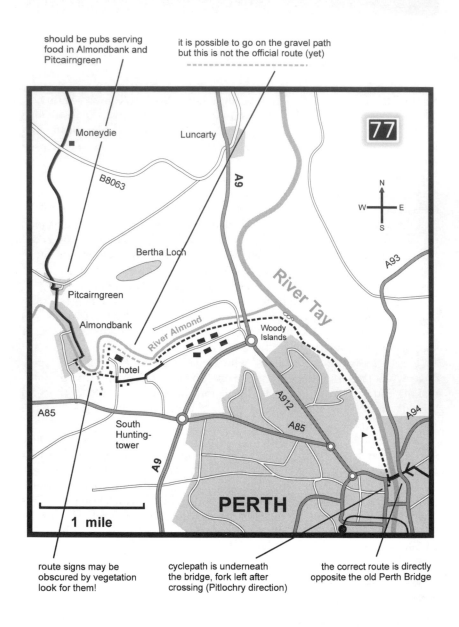

route signs may be
obscured by vegetation
look for them!

cyclepath is underneath
the bridge, fork left after
crossing (Pitlochry direction)

the correct route is directly
opposite the old Perth Bridge

PERTH TO MONEYDIE

In Perth you cross the River Tay using the historic old Perth Bridge. It was built in 1771 by John Smeaton architect of the Eddystone Lighthouse. It's still a working bridge so watch out for the cars. Going west bear left at the far end – the cyclepath is under the bridge. From now on the route in Perth is entirely in a public park, so if you want to explore Perth or buy something do it now!

The cyclepath runs across the North Inch golf course by the River Tay. This has been a golf course for a long time; in 1599 one Laurence Cuthbert was fined for playing golf on the North Inch on the sabbath. There are open views across the River Tay which is quite wide at this point. After a couple of miles the route leaves the Tay and starts to follow the River Almond. It dips under the railway line to Inverness, then under the A9 dual carriageway. It then runs between the river and an industrial estate. A screen of trees has recently been planted and mostly it's quite pleasant. Shortly after this the cyclepath takes a sharp turn and you emerge on to a minor road. It's planned that eventually the route will continue further by the river (grey dotted line on map), but in the meantime follow the signs.

Care is needed as the route between the cyclepath section and Almondbank is a little complex. It is well signposted but some may be obscured by trees etc. There are plenty of signs so if you aren't seeing any go back – you've taken a wrong turning! You cross the River Almond on a metal footbridge. In Almondbank the route passes a small shop which sells food, newspapers etc. There is also a hotel which does bar lunches but this is slightly off route in the main street.

Pitcairngreen is only a short distance to the north. This is an attractive village with a large village green. There is also a village inn. At the time of writing it was being enlarged to include a restaurant so by the time you read this a bar lunch should be a possibility. North of Pitcairngreen the route is very rural: there are no food stops between Pitcairngreen and Bankfoot. There was a stone circle at Moneydie but the last stone was removed by the farmer in 1960.

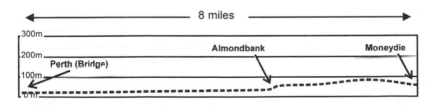

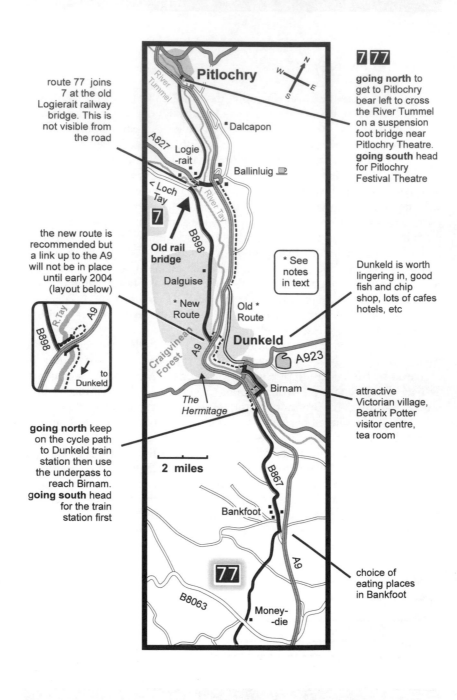

route 77 joins 7 at the old Logierait railway bridge. This is not visible from the road

the new route is recommended but a link up to the A9 will not be in place until early 2004 (layout below)

going north keep on the cycle path to Dunkeld train station then use the underpass to reach Birnam. **going south** head for the train station first

7 **77**

going north to get to Pitlochry bear left to cross the River Tummel on a suspension foot bridge near Pitlochry Theatre. **going south** head for Pitlochry Festival Theatre

Dunkeld is worth lingering in, good fish and chip shop, lots of cafes hotels, etc

attractive Victorian village, Beatrix Potter visitor centre, tea room

choice of eating places in Bankfoot

Pitlochry

River Tummel

Dalcapon

A827

Logie -rait

Ballinluig

< Loch Tay

7

River Tay

B898

Old rail bridge

Dalguise

* New Route

Old * Route

* See notes in text

Dunkeld

A923

Craigvinean Forest

A9

The Hermitage

Birnam

B867

2 miles

Bankfoot

A9

77

B8063

Money- -die

R. Tay

A9

B898

to Dunkeld

MONEYDIE TO PITLOCHRY

Bankfoot is a small place; being near the main road north it has developed to serve traffic going to the Highlands. There are places to eat, a visitor centre and food shops. Dunkeld six miles further north is more attractive so if I was planning anything more than a bite to eat, I'd press on to Dunkeld. North of Bankfoot, when you meet the A9 continue along the cyclepath beside it to the train station where there is an underpass – you emerge in Birnam. Birnam is a very attractive Victorian village (Beatrix Potter visitor centre and tea room) next door to Dunkeld.

Dunkeld has a bike shop, hotels, B&Bs, tea rooms and a cathedral and is in a beautiful situation beside the River Tay. The town with its restored seventeenth-century houses is worth exploring. Another place of interest might be the Taybank Hotel, where Scots fiddle music may be heard. There are lovely picnic spots.

The current route north of Dunkeld is to the east of the River Tay, however this is forecast to change and the route will be via the B898. The old route is beside the A9 main road so isn't very pleasant. The new route will be signposted when open but you've been able to cycle that way for years. The only part awaiting completion is a ramp and footway at the A9 Tay Bridge. At the east end of Dunkeld main street, go left through a wide gate with turrets near a car park, keep going north by the river past Dunkeld House Hotel. When you see the main road go under the bridge, up the bank then turn right to cross the River Tay on the footway beside the A9 (take care), then join the B898.

Route 77 meets Route 7 at the Logierait Bridge. This is obscured by trees; the track to it is near a stone cottage with two chimneys and three chimney pots. Going north from the bridge turn left on to the A827 for 300 metres then sharp right to a minor road near the Logierait Hotel. After this it's four miles on a hilly little road to Pitlochry. In Pitlochry the route uses a footbridge over the River Tummel near Pitlochry Festival Theatre to get to the town centre. For more information on Pitlochry see page 99.

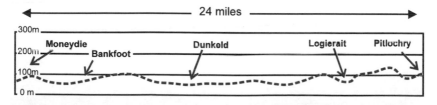

APPENDIX

PLACES TO STAY

This is a list of places to stay along the routes. The main location is in bold. Some readers assume that I've personally checked out every B&B in the list but I've quite enough to do trying to get the route descriptions right. I did however spend two days phoning B&B owners in the list. Many said that they have had a lot of cyclists and they like having you.

Glasgow Youth Hostel
7–8 Park Terrace
Glasgow G3 6BY
0870 004 1119

Glasgow Backpackers
17 Park Terrace
Glasgow G3 6BX
0141 332 9099

Blue Sky Hostel
65 Berkerley Street
Glasgow G3 7DX
0141 221 1710

Mr and Mrs Paterson (B&B)
16 Bogton Avenue
Glasgow G44 3JJ
0141 637 4402

Heritage Guest House
5 Alfred Terrace
Glasgow G12 8RS
0141 339 6955

Kelvin Hotel
15 Buckingham Terrace
Great Western Road
Glasgow G12 8EB
0141 339 7143

Number 36 (GH)
36 St Vincent Crescent
Glasgow G3 8NG
0141 248 2086

Manor Park Hotel
28 Balshagray Drive
Broomhill
Glasgow G11 7DD
0141 339 2143

Tourist Information
11 George Square
Glasgow G2 1DY
0141 204 4400

Tourist Information
9a Gilmour Street
Paisley
0141 889 0711

Mrs W Campbell B&B
Ferguslea, 98 New Road
Ayr KA8 8JG
01292 268551
Chaz Ann B&B
17 Park Circus
Ayr KA7 2DJ
01292 611215

Horizon Hotel
Esplanade,
Ayr KA7 1DT
01292 264384

Tourist Information
Burns House
Burns Statue Square
Ayr
01292 678100

Homelea (B&B)
62 Culzean Road
Maybole KA19 8AH
01655 882736

Garpin Farm (B&B)
Crosshill
by **Maybole** KA19 7PX
01655 740214

Minnigaff Youth Hostel
Newton Stewart
DG8 6PL
0870 004 1142

Miss K Wallace (B&B)
6 Auchendoon Road
Newton Stewart
DG8 6HD
01671 402818

Benera (B&B)
Corsbie Road
Newton Stewart
DG8 6JD
01671 403443

Flowerbank Guest House
Millcroft Road
Minnigaff
Newton Stewart
DG8 6PJ
01671 402629

Tourist Information
Dashwood Square
Newton Stewart
01671 402431

Jean Clements (B&B)
48 Catherine Street
Gatehouse of Fleet
DG7 2JB
01557 814826

Murray Arms Hotel
Ann Street
Gatehouse of Fleet
DG7 2DW
01557 814207

Tourist Information
Car Park
Gatehouse of Fleet
01557 814212

Mrs Watson (B&B)
Boreland of Borgue
Twynholm
Kirkcudbright DG6 4SX
01557 860214

Miriam Baker (B&B)
3 High Street
Kirkcudbright
01557 330881

Marie McLaughlin (B&B)
14 High Street
Kirkcudbright
01557 330766

Don and Pam Inman (B&B)
Millburn House
Millburn Street
Kirkcudbright DG6 4ED
01557 339166

Jennifer Baty (B&B)
31 Castle Street
Kirkcudbright DG6 4JT.
01557 330351

Tourist Information
Harbour Square
Kirkcudbright
01557 330494

Galloway Sailing Centre
Loch Ken Parton
(hostel, 5 miles north of)
Castle Douglas DG7 3NQ
01644 420626

M Laidlaw (B&B)
33 Abercromby Road
Castle Douglas DG7 1BA
01556 503103

Mrs P E Kirk (B&B)
49 Ernespie Road
Castle Douglas DG7 1LD
01556 502360

The Crown Hotel
25 King Street
Castle Douglas DG7 1AA
01556 502031

Tourist Information
Markethill Car Park
Castle Douglas
01556 502611

Marilyn McNeish (B&B)
47 Glebe Street
Dumfries DG1 2LZ
01387 255280

Mrs McRae (B&B)
23 Rae Street
Dumfries DG1 1HY
01387 264076

Glenaldor House (B&B)
5 Victoria Terrace
Dumfries DG1 1NL
01387 264248

Torbay Lodge (B&B)
31 Lovers Walk
Dumfries DG1 1LR
01387 253922

Aberdour Hotel
16–20 Newall Terrace
Dumfries DG1 1LW
01387 252060

Tourist Information
Whitesands
Dumfries
01387 253862

Mrs Forrest (B&B)
Hurkledale Farm
Cummertrees by **Annan**
DG12 5QA
01461 700228

Mrs R. Robinson (B&B)
Milnfield Farm
Low Road
Annan DG12 5QP
01461 201811

Corner House Hotel
78 High Street
Annan DG12 6DL
01461 202754

Mrs V. Greenhow (B&B)
166 Central Avenue
Gretna DG16 5AF
01461 337533

Carol Welsh (B&B)
The Beeches
Loanwath Road
off Sarkfoot Road
Gretna DG16 5EP
01461 337448

Rod and Celia Duncan
(B&B)
Thistlewood, Rigg
Gretna DG16 5JQ
01461 337810

Tourist Information
Blacksmith's Shop
Gretna Green
01461 337834

Avondale B&B
3 St Aidens Road
Carlisle CA1 1LT
01228 523012

Tourist Information
Old Town Hall
Carlisle
01228 625600

Lynbank Hotel
Lynebank, **West Linton**
by **Carlisle** (5 miles north)
CA6 6AA
01228 792820

Abbey Court Guest Hse.
24 London Road
Carlisle CA1 2EL
01228 528696

CHAPTER 3: EDINBURGH–GLASGOW

Bruntsfield Youth Hostel
7–8 Bruntsfield Crescent
Edinburgh EH10 4EZ
0131 447 2994

Castle Park Guest House
75 Gilmore Place
Edinburgh EH3 9NU
0131 229 1215

Rosslea Guest House
107 Forrest Street
Airdrie ML6 7AR
01236 765865

Eglinton Youth Hostel
18 Eglinton Crescent
Edinburgh EH12 5DD
0131 337 1120

Galloway Guest House
22 Dean Park Crescent
Edinburgh EH4 1PH
0131 332 3672

Georgian Hotel
26 Lefroy Street
Coatbridge ML5 1LZ
01236 421888

High Street Hostel
8 Blackfriars Street
Edinburgh EH1 1NE
0131 557 3984

Tourist Information
3 Princess Street
Edinburgh
0131 473 3800

Glasgow Youth Hostel
7–8 Park Terrace
Glasgow G3 6BY
0870 004 1119

Castle Rock Hostel
15 Johnstone Terrace
Edinburgh EH1 2PW
0131 225 9666

Mrs M Connell (B&B)
35 The Green
Bathgate EH48 4DA
01506 654830

Tourist Information
11 George Square
Glasgow G2 1DY
0141 204 4400

Burns (B&B)
67 Gilmore Place
Edinburgh EH3 9NU
0131 229 1669

Mr and Mrs Aitken (B&B)
108 Lauchope Street
Chapelhall
Airdrie ML6 8SW
01236 753774
(1 mile south of route)

FOR MORE
SUGGESTIONS IN
GLASGOW SEE THE
BEGINNING OF THE
GLASGOW–CARLISLE
SECTION

CHAPTER 4: GLASGOW–INVERNESS

Glasgow Youth Hostel
7–8 Park Terrace
Glasgow G3 6BY
0870 004 1119

Tourist Information
11 George Square
Glasgow G2 1DY
0141 204 4400

FOR MORE
SUGGESTIONS IN
GLASGOW SEE THE
BEGINNING OF THE
GLASGOW–CARLISLE
SECTION

Mrs M Murphy (B&B)
10 Drumry Road
Clydebank G81 2LJ
0141 941 3171

Kilmalid House (B&B)
17 Glenpath, Barnhill Road
Dumbarton G82 2QL
01389 732030

Gowanlea Guest House
Drymen Road
Balloch G83 8HS
01389 752456

Balloch House
Balloch Road
Balloch G83 8LQ
01389 752579

Easter Drumguhassle Farm
Gartness Road
Drymen
(B&B) & Wigwams
01360 660893

Mrs Epps (B&B)
Crannaig House
Trossachs Road
Aberfoyle FK8 3SR
01877 382276

Mrs Haighton (B&B)
Stoneypark
Loch Ard Road
Aberfoyle FK8 3SZ
01877 382208

Tourist Information
Main Street
Aberfoyle
01877 382352

Trossachs Backpackers
(+ Wheels cycle shop/hire)
Invertrossachs Road
Callander FK17 8HW
01877 331200

Coppice Hotel
Leny Road
Callander FK17 8AL
01877 330188

Tourist Information
Ancaster Square
Callander
01877 330342

Killin Youth Hostel
Killin FK2 8TN
01567 820546

Drumfinn Guest House
Manse Road
Killin FK21 8UY
01567 829900

Breadalbane (B&B)
Main Street
Killin FK21 8UT
01567 820134

Invertay House (B&B)
Killin FK21 8TN
01567 820492

Killin Hotel
Killin FK21 8TP
01567-820296
(excellent for food)

The Kenmore Hotel
The Square
Kenmore PH15 2NU
01887 830205

Caber Feidh Guest House
Dunkeld Street
Aberfeldy PH15 2AF
01887 820342

Tourist Information
The Square
Aberfeldy
01887 829495

Pitlochry Youth Hostel
Knockard Road
Pitlochry PH16 5HJ
01796 472308

Mrs Sheila Bryson (B&B)
Highlands
Ferry Road
Pitlochry PH16 5DD
01796 474469

Mrs Cochrane (B&B)
5 Lettoch Terrace
Pitlochry PH16 5BA
01796 472152

Atholl Centre (B&B)
Atholl Road
Pitlochry PH16 5BX
01796 473044

Craigmhor Lodge (B&B)
27 West Moulin Road
Pitlochry PH16 5EF
01796 472123

Tourist Information
22 Atholl Road
Pitlochry
01796 472215

Beechwood (B&B)
The Terrace
Blair Atholl PH18 5SZ
01796 481379

Dalgreine (GH)
St Andrews Crescent
Blair Atholl PH18 5SZ
01796 481276

The Firs (B&B)
St Andrews Crescent
Blair Atholl PH18 5TA
01796 481256

Loch Ericht Hotel
Dalwhinnie
PH19 1AF
01528 522257

Newtonmore Hostel
Main Street
Newtonmore PH20 1DA
01540 673360
(Bike repairs too!)

Strathspey Mountain
Hostel, Main Street
Newtonmore PH20
01540 673694

Glenquoich House (B&B)
Glen Road
Newtonmore
PH20 1EB
01540 673461

Tom An T'Silidh (B&B)
Station Road
Newtonmore
PH20 1AR
01540 673554

Tourist Information
Ralia, by **Newtonmore**
Inverness-shire
01540 673253

The Laird's Bothy (hostel)
High Street
Kingussie PH21 1HZ
01540 661334

Homewood Lodge (B&B)
Newtonmore Road
Kingussie PH21 1HD
01540 661507

Rowan House (B&B)
Homewood
Newtonmore Road
Kingussie PH21 1HD
01540 662153

Avondale Guest House
Newtonmore Road
Kingussie PH21 1HF
01540 661731

Bothan Airigh Bunkhouse
Insh
by **Kingussie** PH21 1NT
01540 661051

Kirkbeag (B&B)
Kincraig
PH21 1ND
01540 651298

Insh Water Sports (B&B)
by **Kincraig**
PH21 1NU
01540 651272

Insh House (B&B)
Kincraig PH21 1NU
01540 651377

Glen Feshie Hostel
Glen Feshie
PH21 1NH
01540 651323
(2 miles off route but free
porridge)

Aviemore Youth Hostel
25 Grampian Road
Aviemore PH22 1PR
01479 810345

Loch Morlich Youth Hostel
Glenmore
by **Aviemore** PH22 1QY
01479 861238
(off route 5 miles)

Vermont Guest House
Grampian Road
Aviemore PH22 1RP
01479 810470

Kinapol Guest House
Dalfaber Road
Aviemore PH22 1PY
01479 810513

Mrs M Fraser (B&B)
35 Strathspey Avenue
Aviemore PH22 1SN
01479 811226

Tourist Information
Grampian Road
Aviemore
01479 810363

Carrbridge Hostel
Carrbridge PH23 3AX
01479 841250

Birchwood (B&B)
12 Rowan Park
Carrbridge PH23 3BE
01479 841393

Fairwinds Hotel
Carrbridge PH23 3AA
01479 841240

Inverness Youth Hostel
Victoria Drive
Inverness IV2 3QB
01463 231771

Eastgate Backpackers
38 Eastgate
Inverness IV2 3NA
01463 718756

Ho Ho Hostel
23a High Street
Inverness IV1 1HY
01463 221225

Ardgowan (B&B)
45 Fairfield Road
Inverness IV3 5QP
01463 236489

Ardconnel House (GH)
21 Ardconnel Street
Inverness IV2 3EU
01463 240455

Aberfeldy Lodge (GH)
11 Southside Road
Inverness IV2 3BG
01463 231120

Tourist Information
Castle Wynd
Inverness
01463 234353

CHAPTER 5: INVERNESS–JOHN O' GROATS

SEE THE END OF THE
GLASGOW–INVERNESS
SECTION FOR
SUGGESTIONS IN
INVERNESS

Beechfield House (B&B)
4 Urquhart Court
Cromarty IV11 8YD
01381 600308

Lower Pitcalnie (B&B)
Nigg, Tain
Ross-shire IV19 1QX
01862 851445

Mrs M. McLean (B&B)
23 Moss Road
Tain IV19 1HH
01862 894087 (£15-19)

Rosslyn B&B
4 Hartfield Gardens
Tain IV19 1DL
01862 892697

Carrington's B&B
Morangie Road
Tain IV19 1PY
01862 892635

Carbisdale Castle
Youth Hostel
Culrain IV24 3DP
01549 421232

Mrs D. Munro (B&B)
Corvost
Ardgay IV24 3BP
01863 755317

Mrs B. M. Paterson (B&B)
Strathwin
Lairg IV27 4AZ
01549 402487

Carnbren (B&B)
Station Road
Lairg IV27 4AY
01549 402259

Crask Inn
by **Lairg** IV27 4AB
01549 411241
(do bar lunches)

Altnaharra Hotel
by **Lairg** IV27 4UE
01549 411222

Tongue Youth Hostel
Tongue
by **Lairg** IV27 4XH
01549 402507

Tongue Hotel
Tongue
by **Lairg** IV27 4XD
01847 611206

Ben Loyal Hotel
Tongue IV27 4XE
01847 611216

Mrs H. I. McPherson (B&B)
7 Borgie, Skerray
by Bettyhill
by **Thurso** KW14 7TH
01641 521428

Tourist Information
Bettyhill
01641 521342

Sandra's Backpackers
24-6 Prince Street
Thurso KW14 7BQ
01847 894575

Murray House (B&B)
1 Campbell Street
Thurso KW14 7HD
01847 895759

Waterside House (B&B)
3 Janet Street
Thurso KW14 7AR
01847 894751

Tourist Information
Thurso
01847 892371

———————————————

John o' Groats Youth Hostel
Canisbay, near **Wick**
KW1 4YH
01463 243402

———————————————

Gaber-feidh (GH)
John o' Groats
KW1 4YR
01955 611219

Seaview Hotel
John o' Groats
KW1 4YR
01955 611220

Tourist Information
John o' Groats
01955 611373

CHAPTER 6: INVERNESS–ABERDEEN

Durham House B&B
4 Academy Street
Nairn IV12 4RJ
01667 452345

Ceol-Mara B&B
Links Place
Nairn IV12 4NH
01667 452495

Glen Lyon Lodge (B&B)
Waverley Road
Nairn IV12 4RH
01667 452780

———————————————

Mrs Jacqui Banks (B&B)
16 Forbes Road
Forres IV36 0HP
01309 674066

———————————————

Saltire Hostel
Pluscarden Road
Elgin IV30 3TE
01343 551467 / 550624

West End Guest House
282 High Street
Elgin IV30 1AG
01343 549629

Moraydale Guest House
276 High Street
Elgin IV30 1AG
01343 546381

Ardgowan B&B
37 Duff Avenue
Elgin IV30 1QS
01343 541993

Tourist Information
17 High Street
Elgin
01343 543388

———————————————

Shona Kemp (B&B)
27 Nether Dallachy
Spey Bay IV32 7PL
01343 821070

C. J. Crawford (B&B)
26 Richmond Terrace
Portgordon by
Buckie AB56 2RJ
01542 833221

Mrs E. MacMillan (B&B)
81 High Street
Buckie AB56 1BB
01542 832367

Sea Breezes Guest House
28 Gordon Street
Portgordon by
Buckie AB56 5QR
01542 833681

———————————————

Mrs M. Phimister (B&B)
13 Ogilvie Park
Cullen AB56 4XZ
01542 840017

Mrs M. Whitelaw (B&B)
1 Cathay Terrace
Cullen AB56 4RX
01542 840152

———————————————

Carmelite House Hotel
Low Street
Banff AB45 1AY
01261 812152

Bryvard Guest House
Seafield Street
Banff AB45 1EB
01261 818090

Trinity and Alvah Manse
((B&B)) 21 Castle Street
Banff AB45 1DH
01261 812244

Mrs I. Wilkie (B&B)
Morayhill
Bellevue Road
Banff AB45 1BJ
01261 815956

Tourist Informatiom
Collie Lodge
Banff
01261 812419

———————————————

W. & M. Stewart (B&B)
The Gables
Station Road
Turriff AB53 4ER
01888 568715

Fife Arms Hotel
The Square
Turriff AB53 4AE
01888 563124

Mr and Mrs Hepburn
Pond View
Brucklay
Maud AB42 4QW
01771 613675

Mrs Rhind (B&B)
Old Bank House
6 Abbey Street
Old Deer AB42 5LN
(3 miles east of **Maud**)
01771 623463

Brackenbrae (B&B)
Ythanbank
Ellon AB41 0TH
01358 761222

Mrs M. Thomson (B&B)
58 Station Road
Ellon AB41 9AL
01358 720263

Station Hotel
Station Brae
Ellon AB41 9BD
01358 720209

Tourist Information
The Square
Huntly (for Maud, Ellon, Tarves etc.)
01466 792255

Linsmohr Hotel
Oldmeldrum Road
Pitmedden
AB41 7NY
01651 842214

Aberdeen Youth Hostel
8 Queens Road
Aberdeen AB15 4ZT
01224 646988

Aldersyde Guest House
138 Bon Accord Street
Aberdeen AB11 6TX
01224 580012

Braeside Guest House
68 Bon Accord Street
Aberdeen AB11 6EL
01224 571471

Lochnagar Guest House
11 Affleck Street
Aberdeen AB11 6JH
01224 575964

Royal Crown Guest House
111 Crown Street
Aberdeen AB11 6HN
01224 586461

Lillian Cottage Guest Hse
442 King Street
Aberdeen AB24 3BS
01224 636947

Tourist Information
27 Albyn Place
Aberdeen AB10 1YL
01224 288825

CHAPTER 7: ABERDEEN–EDINBURGH

SEE THE END OF THE
INVERNESS–ABERDEEN
SECTION FOR
SUGGESTIONS IN
ABERDEEN

Mo Sangster (B&B)
9 Dunnottar Avenue
Stonehaven AB39 2JD
01569 762612

The Grahams (B&B)
71 Cameron Street
Stonehaven AB39 2HE
01569 763517

Mrs Miriam Malcolm (B&B)
Beachgate House
Beachgate Lane
Stonehaven AB39 2BD
01569 763155

Heugh Hotel
Westfield Road
Stonehaven AB39 2EE
01569-762379

Tourist Information
66 Allardice Street
Stonehaven
01569 762806

The Limes Guest House
15 King Street
Montrose DD10 8NL
01674 677236

Oaklands Guest House
10 Rossie Island Road
Montrose DD10 9NN
01674 672018

Tourist Information
Bridge Street
Montrose
01674 672000

Mrs W. Brookes (B&B)
7 Helen Street
Arbroath DD11 3AP
01241 874912

Blairdene Guest House
216 High Street
Arbroath DD11 1HY
01241 872380

Mrs M. Fergusson (B&B)
20 Hillend Road
Arbroath DD11 2AR
01241 873991

Tourist Information
Market Place
Arbroath
01241 872609

Riverview Backpackers
127 Broughty Ferry Rd
Dundee DD4 6LB
01382 450565

Cullaig Guest House
Upper Constitution Street
Dundee DD3 6JQ
01382 322154

Nelson Guest House
8 Nelson Terrace
Dundee DD1 2PR
01382 225354

Ash Villa Guest House
216 Arbroath Road
Dundee DD4 7RZ
01382 450831

Tourist Information
7–21 Castle Street
Dundee
01382 527527

Mrs M. Hunter (B&B)
30 Drumcarrow Road
St Andrews KY16 8SE
01334 472036

Mrs J. P. Joy (B&B)
38 Chamberlain Street
St Andrews KY16 8JF
01334 473749

Lorimer House (B&B)
19 Murray Park
St Andrews KY16 9AW
01334 476599

Tourist Information
70 Market Street
St Andrews
01334 472021

Falkland Hostel
The Burgh Lodge
Backwynd
Falkland KY15 7BX
01337 857710

Covenanter Hotel
The Square
Falkland KY15 7BU
01337 857224

Parkview (B&B)
7 Park Place
Dunfermline KY12 7JQ
01383 737187

Tourist Information
13–15 Maygate
Dunfermline
01383 720999

The Priory (B&B)
East End
Star of Markinch
01592 754566

Morven (B&B)
Victoria Road
Markinch
01592 755692

Gamekeeper's Cottage
(B&B)
Balbirnie Park
Markinch
01592 612742

Mrs C. Ketchion (B&B)
69 Lady Nairn Avenue
Kirkcaldy KY1 2AR
01592 652806

Scotties (B&B)
213 Nicol Street
Kirkcaldy KY1 1PF
01592 268596

Mrs E. Duncan (B&B)
20 Southerton Road
Kirkcaldy KY2 5NB
01592 643673

Parkway Hotel
6 Abbotshall Road
Kirkcaldy KY2 5PQ
01592 262143

Tourist Information
19 Whytecauseway
Kirkcaldy
01592 267775

SEE THE START OF
THE
EDINBURGH–GLASGOW
SECTION FOR
SUGGESTIONS IN
EDINBURGH

CHAPTER 8: EDINBURGH–BERWICK ON TWEED

SEE THE START OF THE EDINBURGH–GLASGOW SECTION FOR SUGGESTIONS IN EDINBURGH

Rathan House (B&B)
45 Eskbank Road
Dalkeith EH22 3BH
0131 663 3291

Mrs J. Caird (B&B)
Traquair Bank
Innerleithen EH44 6PS
01896 830425

St Ronan's Hotel
High Street
Innerleithen EH44 6HF
01896 831487

Caddon View Hotel
14 Pirn Road
Innerleithen EH44 6HH
01896 830208

Traquair Arms Hotel
Traquair Road
Innerleithen EH44 6PD
01896 830229

Melrose Youth Hostel
Priorwood
Melrose TD6 9EF
01896 822521

Braidwood (B&B)
Buccleuch Street
Melrose TD6 9LD
01896 822488

Dunfermline GH
Buccleuch Street
Melrose TD6 9LB
01896 822148

Tourist Information
Abbey House
Melrose
08706 080404

Bellevue House (B&B)
Bowmont Street
Kelso TD5 7DZ
01573 224588

Cross Keys Hotel
36–7 The Square
Kelso TD5 7HL
01573 223303

Tourist Information
The Square
Kelso
08706 080404

Mrs D. Jenkins (B&B)
I Leet Street
Coldstream TD12 4BJ
01890 883047

Garth House (B&B)
7 Market Street
Coldstream TD12 4BU
01890 882477

Tourist Information
High Street
Coldstream
08706 080404

Orkney House (GH)
37 Woolmarket
Berwick on Tweed
TD15 1DH
01289 331710

Sandra Thornton (B&B)
4 North Road
Berwick on Tweed
TD15 1PL
01289 306146

Jean Booth (B&B)
6 North Road
Berwick on Tweed
TD15 1PL
01289 308949

Cloverlee B&B
58 West Street
Berwick on Tweed
TD15 1AS
01289 302337

Tourist Information
106 Marygate
Berwick on Tweed
01289 330733

CHAPTER 9: DUNDEE–PITLOCHRY

Riverview Backpackers
127 Broughty Ferry Road
Dundee DD4 6LB
01382 450565

Cullaig Guest House
Upper Constitution Street
Dundee DD3 6JQ
01382 322154

Nelson Guest House
8 Nelson Terrace
Dundee DD1 2PR
01382 225354

Ash Villa Guest House
216 Arbroath Road
Dundee DD4 7RZ
01382 450831

Tourist Information
7–21 Castle Street
Dundee
01382-527527

Albert Villa Guest Hse
63 Dunkeld Road
Perth PH1 5RP
01738 622730

Almond Villa Guest Hse
51 Dunkeld Road
Perth PH1 5RP
01738 629356

Park Lane Guest Hse
17 Marshall Place
Perth PH2 8AG
01738 637218

Pitlochry Youth Hostel
Knockard Road
Pitlochry
PH16 5IIJ
01796 472308

Mrs Sheila Bryson (B&B)
Highlands
Ferry Road
Pitlochry PH16 5DD
01796 474469

Mrs Cochrane (B&B)
5 Lettoch Terrace
Pitlochry PH16 5BA
01796 472152

Atholl Centre (B&B)
Atholl Road
Pitlochry PH16 5BX
01796 473044

Craigmhor Lodge (B&B)
27 West Moulin Road
Pitlochry PH16 5EF
01796 472123

Tourist Information
22 Atholl Road
Pitlochry
01796 472215

CYCLE HIRE

You can rent mountain bikes in very many places in Scotland but the following shops offer a wide range of cycles. Local tourist offices should also be able to put you in touch with cycle hirers (see accommodation lists).

Dales Cycles	Bike Trax Cycle Hire	Edinburgh Cycle Hire
Dobbies Loan	13 Lochrin Place	29 Blackfriars Street
Glasgow G3 0JE	**Edinburgh** EH3 9QX	**Edinburgh**
0141 332 2705	0131 228 6633	0131 556 5560

PUBLIC TRANSPORT

TRAINS For train information phone 0845 484850. If you are using the train to plan a long cycle trip it is advisable to book a bike space well in advance.
For information on cycle carriage on Scotrail trains see
www.scotrail.co.uk/cycle.htm
For GNER: 08457 225225 or www.gner.co.uk/bikes.html
For Virgin: 08457 222333

BUSES Buses in Scotland do not generally carry bikes unless they are partly taken apart and contained in a bike box. Sometimes in rural areas drivers may oblige but you cannot rely on this.

SUSTRANS

Sustrans – it stands for sustainable transport – is a charity that works on practical projects to encourage people to walk, cycle and use public transport in order to reduce motor traffic and its adverse effects.

National Cycle Network Centre
2 Cathedral Square
Bristol
BS1 5DD
0845 113 0065
www.nationalcyclenetwork.org.uk

Sustrans Scotland
162 Fountainbridge
Edinburgh EH3 7AA
0131 624 7660

OTHER USEFUL ADDRESSES

P&O Scottish Ferries
Jamieson's Quay
Aberdeen AB10 1YL
(Orkney ferry)
01224 288800

John o' Groats Ferries
John o' Groats KW1 4YR
01955 611353

Caledonian MacBrayne
Hebridean & Clyde Ferries
The Ferry Terminal
Gourock 0990 650000
www.calmac.co.uk

Spokes
Lothian Cycle Campaign
232 Dalry Road
Edinburgh EH11 2JG
0131 313 2114
www.spokes.org.uk

Scottish Youth Hostels Association
7 Glebe Crescent
Stirling FK8 2JA
01786 891400
www.syha.org.uk

Visit Scotland
23 Ravelston Terrace
Edinburgh EH4 3EU
0131 332 2433
www.cycling.visitscotland.com

Fife Millennium Cycle Ways
Fife House
North Street
Glenrothes KY7 5LT
01592 413043
www.fife-cycleways.co.uk